JOHNNY
CAN'T
WRITE

WHY JOHNNY CAN'T WRITE

HOW TO IMPROVE WRITING SKILLS

Myra J. Linden
Art Whimbey

1990

LAWRENCE ERLBAUM ASSOCIATES, PUBLISHERS
Hillsdale, New Jersey   Hove and London

Lawrence Erlbaum Associates, Inc., Publishers
365 Broadway
Hillsdale, New Jersey 07642

Library of Congress Catalog-in-Publication Data

Linden, Myra J.
Why Johnny can't write : how to improve writing skills / Myra J.
Linden, Arthur Whimbey.
p.   cm.
Includes bibliographical references and indexes.
ISBN 0-8058-0852-3. — ISBN 0-8058-0853-1 (pbk.)
1. English language—Composition and exercises—Study and
teaching.   I. Whimbey, Arthur.   II. Title.
PE1404.L54   1990
808'.042'07—dc20   90-39836
                                                                CIP

Printed in the United States of America
10 9 8 7 6 5 4

We dedicate this book to the long, healthy life of the National Writing Project and its affiliates. In particular, we thank Eveleen Lorton and the other teachers of the Dade County Public Schools/University of Miami Writing Institute for their friendship, support, and stimulating experiences.

Contents

CHAPTER 1

Johnny's Country
Is Losing Business

What is the cost of illiterate and semi-literate American workers? Benjamin Franklin warned in *Poor Richard's Almanac*:

> A little neglect may breed mischief . . . for want of a nail, the shoe was lost; for want of a shoe, the horse was lost; and for want of a horse, the rider was lost.

The warning forebodes calamity when, for want of the rider, the battle is lost; and for want of the battle, the country is lost. It is beginning to appear that for want of literate American workers, an updated version of this adage may run along these lines:

> For want of literacy skills, workers are lost; for want of workers, profits and companies are lost; for want of competitive companies, markets are lost; for want of markets, the country's economy is being helped to hell; and all for the want of literacy skills.

In a *Boston Globe* article, Professor Chall of Harvard reveals that over half of the adults in this country are unqualified for today's technical jobs because of their lack of reading and writing skills. At the same time the Bureau of Census reports that beginning in the 1990s the nation will start to experience labor shortages. The pool of 18–24-year-old workers will shrink from 30 million in 1980 to only 24 million in 1995 according to its projections. With 44% of American students not continuing their education past the high school level and

1

job requirements steadily rising, employers will face critical shortages of qualified workers.

The Grant Foundation Commission on Work, Family, and Citizenship presents another view of the problem. According to its studies, high school students in the lowest 20% of their classes in basic skills are nearly nine times more likely to drop out and to be unmarried parents as those in the top half of their classes. Also, they are five times more likely to live eventually in poverty and over twice as likely to be arrested in a given year.

Writing is one of the basic skills which American students are not mastering. According to *The Writing Report Card* (the most recent report from the National Assessment of Educational Progress) only 25% of 11th graders write well enough to receive a rating of "adequate" in the type of writing required for educational advancement or business and technical work; 75% write inadequately.

The inability of our schools to prepare students adequately for employment is forcing American businesses to spend $25 billion a year teaching employees basic skills. Ford is spending $50 million a year on education, including teaching 8,000 employees how to read and write. Motorola spends an equal amount teaching half of its hourly employees seventh-grade English and mathematics. Chrysler spent $11 million in 1988 alone to teach literacy skills. And General Motors advertises that it now has the largest private education program in the world, a joint effort with the United Auto Workers union.

More money for education is not the sole answer. According to the *Washington Post,* America already ranks first in the world in educational spending, although much lower in educational achievement. But two new methods for teaching writing skills may be a major part of the answer.

Two recently developed methods for teaching writing skills have been found not only to improve all aspects of writing—ranging from spelling and grammar to logical organization—but also to strengthen reading ability, which could have enormous benefits for our entire educational system. The two methods have been developed within the past 20 years but are not yet widely used because of traditions and misunderstanding. This book will explain the two new methods. It will also explain why some methods still widely used for teaching writing in our schools have proven ineffective.

You should find this book interesting and useful if you are a teacher, parent, taxpayer, or employer concerned with American education, and writing and reading skills in particular.

You will also find this book worthwhile if you are reading it to improve your own writing skills. You will learn which approaches to use and which to avoid, which build skills quickly and which have proved to be just boring busy work. Furthermore, doing the sample exercises included in most chapters will strengthen your writing skills and provide a solid foundation for your life-long program of language growth.

CHAPTER 2

Grammar: The Ineffectual Monster

The boredom or terror of grammar is the first association that comes to mind when many youngsters and adults think of English class. They shudder from the endless grammatical terms—indefinite pronouns, intransitive verb, participle, gerund, adverbial phrase—that must be memorized and used in labeling the words of sentences or taking sentences apart in diagrams:

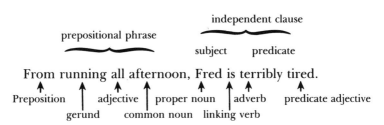

Grammar study is not just an unhappy memory from the past like World War II or the McCarthy era. The most recent survey of writing instruction in America by the National Council of Teachers of English (NCTE), published under the title *Research in Written Composition*, reports that "many elementary and secondary schools continue to make grammar a major component of their curricula" (1986).

For countless students, grammar is a confusing maze leading to tears, tedium, and the total rejection of English classes. The tragedy is that their negative feelings are fully justified.

Sometimes good medicine tastes vile, like fish oil to unclog arteries

or barium for an intestinal x-ray. Sometimes useful exercise is tedious—practicing scales for piano virtuosity, track work to win football
games, and sit-ups for a trim waistline. But it does not follow that all
unpleasant or tedious prescriptions are beneficial.

In 1963 the NCTE published its first comprehensive survey of
research on the teaching of writing. After reviewing all available studies, the authors issued this unequivocal condemnation of grammar
instruction:

> . . . in view of the widespread agreement of research studies based upon
> many types of students and teachers, the conclusion can be stated in
> strong and unqualified terms: the teaching of formal grammar has a
> negligible or, because it usually displaces some instruction and practice
> in actual composition, even a harmful effect on the improvement of
> writing . . .

The most recent NCTE (National Council of Teachers of English)
survey of research finds no reason to question this condemnation:

> None of the studies reviewed for the present report provides any
> support for teaching grammar as a means of improving composition
> skills. If schools insist upon teaching the identification of parts of speech,
> the parsing or diagramming of sentences, or other concepts of tradi-
> tional school grammar (as many still do), they cannot defend it as a
> means of improving the quality of writing.

The thoroughness with which the issue has been researched is seen
from a study by Harris[1] entitled "An Experimental Inquiry into the
Functions and Value of Formal Grammar in the Teaching of English,
with Special Reference to the Teaching of Correct Written English to
Children Aged Twelve to Fourteen." Papers written by a group of
students who studied traditional grammar for two years were compared with papers from students who received no grammar instruction. The papers of students who studied grammar had more errors
and less sentence complexity—that is, they were worse—than the papers from students who were not given grammar instruction. Ironically, the students who studied grammar did master the terminology
and could apply it in analyzing sentences, but this did not have a
positive effect on their actual writing. Other researchers studied stu-

---

[1] Throughout the text we refer by last name to educators whose ideas we cite. Their
publications and other resources are listed in the bibliography.

dents ranging from elementary school to college level—but always with basically the same negative outcome.

Despite fifty years of research showing that learning the parts of speech and identifying them in sentences have no benefits, textbooks continue to feature grammar, as shown by a sample page from one of the best-selling kindergarten-through-eighth-grade language-arts series, *Silver Burdett English* (see Fig. 1). The page in Figure 1 is reprinted from an advertising brochure we picked up at the publisher's table while attending the 1989 convention of the Florida Council of Teachers of English. It is presented in the brochure as representative of the grammar lessons in the seventh-grade-level textbook from the series, as indicated by the statement above the page from the brochure.

Several reasons that grammar instruction has not been useful are illustrated by the lesson. To begin, the terminology involved, such as *interrogative and indefinite pronouns,* is often more complex than the actual sentences it is supposed to help clarify. Count the number of syllables in a random sample of words in this book or any other typical text. You will find most words have one or two syllables. A few have three. However, *interrogative* has five. *Antecedent, infinitive, preposition,* and *adverbial* each has four. Grammatical terms have been overgenerously endowed by their creator with syllables. Large dosages of polysyllabic terminology in teaching any subject produces cognitive overload, jams processing, and hinders learning.

Another problem is limited usage. The terminology of football can be confusing, and terms such as *offside* or *man in motion* stump the novice fan. But these terms are used over and over again at each game, so they eventually become familiar. In contrast, the terms *interrogative* and *indefinite pronoun* are not encountered over and over again in normally using language—in reading magazines, newspapers, or novels ("Sweetheart, the way you whisper interrogative pronouns gives me shivers.")—so the terms have no opportunity to take root in memory.

Furthermore, someone can point out a player *offside* and explain that it means the player is in front of the ball before the hike. Once seen, this is easy to recognize again. But the lesson on *indefinite pronouns* requires memorizing all twenty-four of the words presented in the box labeled "Indefinite Pronouns."

Worse yet, in contrast to seeing a *man in motion,* definitions of grammatical terms invariably involve other complexities and abstract concepts. In the lesson, the five *interrogative pronouns* are illustrated with sentences. The first sentence contains *who* and the last *whom.* Does the lesson explain when to use *whom* instead of who? Deciding which to use requires mastering an entirely different, com-

All lessons in Books 7 and 8 have a predictable, manageable length for easy lesson planning.

---

6 — Interrogative and Indefinite Pronouns

- An **interrogative pronoun** asks a question.
- An **indefinite pronoun** does not always indicate a definite person, place, or thing.

Interrogative Pronouns Interrogative pronouns are often used to begin questions. There are only five, and they all begin with *w*: *who, whose, whom, which,* and *what*. The interrogative pronouns are underlined in the sentences below.

Who has my camera?   What is a tripod?
Whose did you borrow?   Which is the lens?
Whom did she photograph?

Indefinite Pronouns A pronoun that does not always indicate a definite person, place, or thing is called an indefinite pronoun. Many indefinite pronouns express the idea of quantity: *all, several, some*. Indefinite pronouns may or may not have antecedents.

With an antecedent: All of the *leaves* are dry.
Without an antecedent: Somebody lost a glove.

Indefinite Pronouns			
all	each	many	one
any	either	neither	several
anybody	everybody	nobody	some
anyone	everyone	none	somebody
anything	everything	no one	someone
both	few	nothing	something

20   GRAMMAR   Interrogative and Indefinite Pronouns

Exercises

A. Write the pronoun in each sentence. Then identify it as *interrogative* or *indefinite*.

1. Who saw the sunrise today?
2. Will the music bother anybody?
3. What is a good solution to the problem?
4. Someone may develop a cure for the common cold.
5. William wanted neither of the gloves.
6. Whom did the chairperson finally appoint as the program director?
7. Which of the three is most nutritious?
8. Whose would the judges really prefer?
9. Wendy knows nothing about the accident.
10. Are both missing again?

B. Write each sentence, using an indefinite pronoun that completes it appropriately. Use no indefinite pronoun more than twice.

11. ____ was in the corridor.
12. Why were ____ dropped from the list?
13. That certainly is not good for ____.
14. ____ of it looks delicious.
15. We could not see ____ of them.
16. That dictionary defines almost ____.
17. ____ seems wrong with the photograph.
18. Have they seen ____ yet?
19. Certainly ____ must be there by now.
20. ____ of them are excellent actors.
21. ____ of the projectors are in use today.
22. A low calorie diet may not be good for ____.
23. ____ of us could have done more.
24. They might not use ____ of it.
25. ____ of the machines had been repaired.

GRAMMAR   Interrogative and Indefinite Pronouns   21

—from Book 7

FIGURE 1. From "Silver-Burdett English K–8: Setting the New Standard" Brochure. Lexington, MA: Silver, Burdett, & Ginn, 1989. Reprinted with permission.

plex lesson in distinguishing the *subject* from the *object* of a verb in a declarative sentence, and then trying to figure out which the pronoun was originally (*subject* or *object*) before the declarative sentence was transformed into an interrogative sentence.

But the most devastating problem surfaces the very first time a student tries to use his knowledge from the lesson to write just one word—the answer to Exercise 11. For Exercise 11 he must choose a word from the box labeled "Indefinite Pronouns" to fill the blank. Two words in the box are *several* and *everybody*. Will either of them fit the sentence in Exercise 11?

Does the lesson explain why *everybody* is a correct answer but *several* is not? Can the reason be that one word is singular and the other plural? No. *Everybody* and *several* both mean more than one person—logically they must both be plural. In fact, *everybody* is more people than *several*, so *everybody* must be "more" plural. Since *everybody* can be used in Exercise 11 but *several* cannot, should we conclude that only "very" plural pronouns are used with the verb *was*?

No, because another pronoun in the box, *someone*, is also a correct answer for Exercise 11. *Someone* is singular, excepting possibly Siamese twins. Apparently some singular pronouns can also be used with the verb *was*.

But we have traveled far beyond the lesson. Singular indefinite pronouns are not distinguished from plural indefinite pronouns in the lesson. In the box, the indefinite pronouns are neatly listed in alphabetical order, not grouped as singular and plural. There is no way to decide—on the basis of the lesson—which indefinite pronouns can be used with the verb *was* in Exercise 11.

When a student tries to do Exercises 11 to 25, he finds that there is no information in the lesson to help him decide which pronouns from the box can be placed in each blank. The lesson assumes students can properly use indefinite pronouns from language habits they bring to the lesson, and its sole accomplishment is having students memorize the group of words called "indefinite pronouns." It has nothing to do with the real writing ability involved in answering Exercises 11–25, ability developed through usage, not memorization of grammatical categories.

The reason that usage overrides grammar in learning English is seen in the answer to why *everybody* can be used with the verb *was* in Exercise 11. We have here a "special case," common in hybrid English which owes its richness for description at concrete and abstract levels to having borrowed the best from several languages and, for the same reason, fails to follow form like pure predictable Latin.

Everybody, although plural, is always used with a singular verb. One sometimes hears the explanation that *everybody* means the whole single group, so it is singular. But why then isn't *all* singular? *All,* the first word in the box of indefinite pronouns, is synonymous with *everybody* in the context of Exercise 11. ("*All* were in the corridor" means the same as "*Everybody* was in the corridor.") So the answer is not in logical grammar but common usage.

The common problem of special cases stemming from common usage is seen in amusing mistakes by toddlers, such as: "Doggie *eated* all his food." The past tense of *eat* is *ate,* not *eated.* This must be individually learned: There is no grammatical principle for going from *eat* to *ate.* It is one of the many irregular verbs which form a mountain of common usage confusion for anyone trying to learn English through formal grammar.

Generally, people learn a language through usage and employ it by habit. Children can speak proper sentences with subjects, verbs, and modifiers long before they come to school. Their inadequacies in writing arise primarily because spoken language—especially when regional or ethnic dialects are involved—differs from standard written English. Standard written English is the national (and even international) language of business, commerce, science, and academic knowledge, so we want children to graduate from American schools equipped to use it effectively. The best way to learn standard written English, research shows, is the same way spoken language is learned, through usage and habit, not through formal grammar.

Various types of grammar are tools for linguists in describing a language. But teaching a grammar of a language has not proved effective for teaching the language to most students.

Why does grammar continue to be taught? It is not because English teachers do not care about students, or worse, want to see them fail. People who become teachers tend to be sensitive men and women who care very much about helping others. The authors of this book have between them spent three-quarters of a century working in education and have never met a teacher who does not care deeply about helping students learn.

One reason is that a few common grammatical terms are a useful part of any educated person's vocabulary. Terms like *noun, verb, subject,* and *predicate* occur frequently enough in nontechnical discussions of language—such as in newspaper or magazine articles and conversations—that they are worth learning. Also, terminology can be helpful in explaining language patterns to students and in correcting their errors. But experience shows that the terminology is best taught when the need for it arises in a usage lesson, as illustrated in Chapter 9.

While a little, properly dispensed grammar instruction is beneficial, we have been administering fatally large doses to many students because of a more basic problem.

Formal grammar instruction has persisted because truly effective alternatives for teaching writing have not been available until recently. When a society has a need to solve an important problem but no solution to meet the need, the situation is rife for superstition, alchemy, charlatanism, and other grabbing-at-straws methods. This is why George Washington was bled to death by doctors trying to cure his pneumonia. His physicians were not negligent or malicious in treating America's greatest hero of that glorious time, but they had no solid medical knowledge to draw on. Their limited science told them to take the worst possible action.

Yet even this cultural heritage does not keep us from making a similar mistake in language education—teaching grammar—because we are in the same situation as the physicians: The science of mass education is young; we lack understanding about many problems and, until recently, had no effective alternatives for teaching writing. A cynic like Twain could maintain that, no matter how refined our philosophy of science becomes, it may remain difficult to act knowledgeably lacking knowledge.

The effective methods for improving writing skills described in later chapters have been perfected into workable form for classroom application only within the past 20 years. They are not yet widely used because of the inertia encountered with any large-scale institutional change. Other activities occupying language arts classes, supported by the availability of textbooks representing huge financial investments, have slowed their acceptance. Petrosky observed that "publishers continue to produce new programs for teaching grammar, including slight modifications of old programs—all of this without much justification except inclination, demand, and money." Several other retarding influences will be reviewed in later chapters to ease the path for the new methods.

CHAPTER 3

Sentence Combining
To Open Options

Dozens of studies over the past 20 years show that sentence combining (SC) exercises are very effective for improving writing skill. SC teaches students how to combine simple sentences into more complex ones. Here is an example:

> Use the word "before" to combine these two sentences into one:
> 1. The pool was drained.
> 2. The bottom was repaired.
>
> Possible Answers:
> a. The pool was drained *before* the bottom was repaired.
> b. *Before* the bottom was repaired, the pool was drained.

Research shows that SC not only improves a student's ability to write mature, informative sentences but also reduces grammatical errors. Furthermore, SC tends to enhance the overall quality of any student paper or essay. And as an extra bonus, several studies indicate that SC can build reading skill. In short, SC strengthens many aspects of a student's capacity to handle written material.

SC exercises are, in a sense, the opposite of traditional grammar exercises. In traditional grammar, students take sentences apart, whereas in SC they put sentences together.

Moreover, in contrast to literature-oriented instruction, SC clearly emphasizes writing, not reading. In the introduction to *The Writer's Options*, a college SC workbook, students are told:

... You will develop writing skills not by analyzing essays, studying grammar, or even reading books about writing, but by writing itself. ... your writing will improve as you learn to express yourself in different ways and then to choose the most effective option.

The Writer's Options was based on research supported by the Exxon Education Foundation in which some students followed a departmental syllabus which covered modes and elements of writing, using *The Harbrace Reader* and *Writing with A Purpose*. Other students just used SC. Here is the authors' summary of the research:

> During the fall of 1976 almost 300 Miami University freshmen participated in a controlled research study designed to test the effectiveness of two teaching methods in improving writing quality. Half of the students, following a traditional method, read and analyzed essays from a college reader and worked closely with a standard college rhetoric; the other half practiced sentence combining exclusively. After 15 weeks, the sentence-combining students wrote original compositions that a panel of experienced college instructors judged to be superior in overall quality to the compositions written by traditionally trained students.

Several formats for SC exercises have been developed. The first successful study using SC was published by O'Hare in 1973. He used "cued" SC exercises such as this one in which four sentences must be combined:

1. Weightlifting is a method.
2. It is a method of *exercising*.
3. Some athletes find it useful. (WHICH)
4. Others claim it leads to sluggishness. (BUT)

Answer:
> Weightlifting is an exercising method which some athletes find useful but others claim leads to sluggishness.

This is called a "cued" format because cues are given to students on how the sentences should be combined. The cues follow these rules:

1. The main sentence is presented first.
2. Words to be inserted are underlined.
3. Words to be deleted are crossed out.
4. Connecting words, such as WHICH, are written in parentheses after the sentence they connect.

5. Punctuation marks which are to be added also appear in parentheses, as is shown by the comma after BECAUSE in this example.

1. Bob was hungry. (BECAUSE . . . ,)
2. He ordered three hamburgers.

Answer:
Because Bob was hungry, he ordered three hamburgers.

Other examples of cued SC exercises can be found in the two books by O'Hare listed in the bibliography. The effectiveness of cued SC is reflected by O'Hare's research. He found that after seventh-graders went through an SC program, their writing was well above that of typical eighth-graders in syntactic maturity—a measure of the richness or complexity of information within sentences.

An alternative to "cued" SC is "open" SC. In open SC exercises, students are not given cues as to how to combine sentences. Instead, they are presented with several sentences which can be combined in a number of ways. Here is an example from the workbook *The Writer's Options:*

1. The referee blew his whistle.
2. The referee called to the team captains.
3. The referee dropped the puck.
4. The referee began the game.

Possible Answers:
The referee blew his whistle, called to the team captains, and then dropped the puck to begin the game.
After blowing his whistle and calling to the team captains, the referee dropped the puck and began the game.

Students are encouraged to try to write several different combinations. Then the sentences written by various students are compared and discussed so that students learn many options for expressing ideas.

The teacher may also explain that longer is not always better, that an occasional short sentence can have a dramatic effect, as illustrated by the last sentence in this sample answer:

After blowing his whistle and calling to the team captains, the referee dropped the puck between two slashing sticks. The game was on.

In open SC, enough simple sentences may be provided to produce an entire paragraph or even an essay. Spaces between groups of sentences in the following example from *The Writer's Options* indicate where one combined sentence may end and another begin, although students can ignore these spaces and combine the sentences as they wish:

HYPNOTISM
1. Franz Mesmer was a physician.
2. Franz Mesmer was from Germany.
3. Franz Mesmer invented hypnotism.
4. Hypnotism was invented in the eighteenth century.

5. Hypnotism remained an amusing gimmick.
6. It remained a gimmick for over a century.
7. The gimmick was for night club acts.
8. The gimmick was for parlor games.

9. Physicians now use hypnotism.
10. Dentists now use hypnotism.
11. Psychiatrists now use hypnotism.
12. Hypnotism is used to treat various ailments.
13. Hypnotism is used to control chronic pain.
14. Hypnotism is used as a replacement for anesthesia.

The importance of comparing and discussing the versions written by different students in open SC cannot be overemphasized. In cued SC, students are shown various ways to combine ideas into sentences. In open SC, discussion and comparison allow students to see the array of possibilities open to them for expressing their own ideas in writing.

Studies reporting positive benefits of SC are legion, ranging from early elementary grades through adult education: For example, in a study of 50 fifth graders, McAfee found that students who used SC exercises scored higher than students in the regular curriculum on a standardized test of written language and on papers that they wrote. Stoddard found that gifted fifth and sixth graders who used SC wrote better than those who followed the regular gifted-education program. Argall found that college freshmen in developmental writing classes who had five weeks of intensive SC showed a 100% decrease in garbled sentence, 21% decrease in comma splices, 31% decrease in sentence fragments, 67% decrease in fused sentences, and 14% decrease in comma errors.

SC has even been found effective in learning a foreign language. Cooper, Morain, and Kalivorda divided college students studying French, German, and Spanish into two groups: One group received the regular audio-lingual instructions and the other practiced SC but did fewer reading selections. The researchers found that SC improved writing skills and enabled students to use more complex sentences in the languages they were studying.

Several studies, such as that by McAfee cited above, indicate that SC can improve reading ability along with writing skills. The SC exercises in a workbook entitled *Analyze, Organize, Write* by Whimbey and Jenkins were designed specifically to improve analytical thinking and reading skills along with writing skills.

One of us (Whimbey) has been researching methods to help students improve reading and reasoning skills for 20 years. His reasoning-improvement workbook entitled *Problem Solving and Comprehension*— co-authored with Jack Lochhead, Director of the Scientific Reasoning Research Institute at the University of Massachusetts, Amherst—is used in a number of programs including Project SOAR (Stress On Analytical Reasoning) at Xavier University, a historically Black college in New Orleans. Since 1978 over 150 minority students have participated in SOAR each summer, averaging gains of 120 points on the Scholastic Aptitude Test (SAT) and three grade levels on the Nelson-Denny Reading Test. Furthermore, Xavier now sends more Black students to medical schools and other professional health programs than any other U.S. college. According to the staff this is partly due to the focus on reasoning and reading improvement in SOAR and other courses.

One of Whimby's reading-improvement workbooks, *Analytical Reading and Reasoning,* contains this paragraph (reprinted from the *Encyclopedia Americana*) followed by the question shown.

> Infectious diseases are the only ones that can be transmitted. They may be spread by infected animals, infected people, or contaminated substances, such as food and water. Infectious diseases that can be transmitted to humans from infected animals are known as zoonoses. Zoonoses may be transmitted by carriers, such as insects; by the bite of an infected animal; by direct contact with an infected animal or its excretions; or by eating animal products.
>
> Zoonoses are:
> a. Insects that carry diseases.
> b. Infected animals that transmit infectious diseases to humans.
> c. Infectious diseases that man gets from animals.
> d. Carriers that transmit infectious diseases.

For this question, high school and college students with poor reading comprehension ability often pick alternative b. When some of them were asked to explain this choice, they said that *animals* and *diseases* are mentioned often, and that animals are in zoos, so they concluded that zoonoses are animals which spread disease.

This answer reflects the cognitive style of students weak in analytical reading and reasoning. Studies show that they tend to skim material and jump to conclusions. They have not developed the mental skill of working step-by-step in accurately interpreting symbols and spelling out relationships. Researchers have labeled them "one-shot thinkers" to describe their cognitive style.

Other students who selected alternative b, explained that they based their answer on the last six words of the third sentence, namely: "infected animals are known as zoonoses." This answer also reflects the cognitive style of nonanalytical thinkers. Their mental habit is to snap up simple bits of information here and there rather than gradually to work through all the material in a paragraph and reconstruct an accurate picture of it.

Several types of SC exercises were designed to help students learn to read and interpret written material appropriately. In one set of exercises, students must carefully read and think about the meaning of two sentences in deciding which conjunction to use for joining them. First, the use of four conjunctions is illustrated.

AND: Used for just adding one piece of information to another.

1. Jack made a salad.
2. Gloria baked a cake.

Combined: Jack made a salad, and Gloria baked a cake.

OR: Used for joining sentences presenting two possibilities.

1. You must make your car payments.
2. The bank will take your car.

Combined: You must make your car payments, or the bank will take your car.

BUT: Used to show a contrast between two ideas.

1. Harold bought some oranges.
2. His wife had told him to buy tangerines.

Combined: Harold bought some oranges, but his wife had told him to buy tangerines.

SO: Used to show a reason-result relation.

1. The car would not start.
2. I took the bus.

Combined: The car would not start, so I took the bus.

Then students are presented pairs of sentences and told to combine them with one of the four conjunctions. (A note not to use AND is included with some pairs, encouraging students to think more fully about the relationships.) Here are three sample exercises.

1. It was a hot summer day.
2. Linda went for a swim in the pool.
Do not use AND.

Combined:

1. Bill and Judy got married.
2. Their parents wanted them to wait another year.
Do not use AND.

Combined:

1. Stronger laws must be passed to stop air pollution.
2. There will be no clean air left to breathe.

Combined:

A second type of SC exercise is intended to teach students to fully process complicated sentences. In the selection on zoonoses above, the answer for the question is contained in the third sentence:

Infectious diseases that can be transmitted to humans from infected animals are known as zoonoses.

This sentence consists of an independent clause and an embedded dependent clause:

Independent: Infectious diseases are known as zoonoses.
Dependent: that can be transmitted to humans from infected animals

That weak readers can comprehend only simple but not complicated sentences parallels the observation made by mathematics educators that weak students can solve only single-step but not multi-step problems. An inability to deal with complicated material is a general characteristic of students weak in analytical reasoning.

To strengthen the capacity of the mind to deal with complicated material, students practice combining simple sentences into complicated ones. Here are two sample exercises. A more complete review of how students gradually learn to combine sentences is presented in Chapter 9.

Exercise 1

Drop the word "Certain" from the first sentence. Also drop "These companies" from the second sentence. Then add the information from the second sentence by using "which."

1. Certain companies should be severely punished.
2. These companies violate anti-pollution laws.

Combined: Companies which violate anti-pollution laws should be severely punished.

Exercise 2

1. Certain infectious diseases are called zoonoses.
2. These infectious diseases are given to humans by animals

Combined: Infectious diseases which are given to humans by animals are called zoonoses.

Such exercises illustrate why studies have found that SC improves reading ability. SC presents a situation encouraging growth of careful interpretation and reflective thinking. Research on learning of all types—whether physical or mental skills—has shown that active participation, with quick and frequent feedback on performance, is needed to optimize improvement. Watching someone else take target practice, or shooting at a target without finding out how close you come to the bull's eye, will not make you an expert marksman. Similarly, when a teacher assigns a lengthy reading selection without ensuring that students actively process the material and get quick feedback on the accuracy of their comprehension, the exercise may do little to improve comprehension ability. SC can be viewed as a high-incentive situation for careful reading and thinking because it presents just a short amount to be read—several sentences—and then requires an immediate response of integrating the ideas into a single sentence which can be checked quickly by comparing answers with another student or an instructor. This is ideal for strengthening the type of precise reading skill required for complicated or technical material.

Are there any disadvantages to using SC? A few studies, such as that by Ney, did fail to find benefits from SC. But such negative results can almost always be traced to the inadequate use of SC. In the Ney study, for example, SC was used for only 10 minutes a day in 27 classes over 11 weeks—a total of just 4½ hours. A study by Jones indicates that 20 hours of SC is required to optimize syntactic growth for college freshmen. Regarding other negative studies, the Hillocks survey of writing instruction states: "The one clear negative report . . . was later rescinded as the researcher admitted that poor teaching was probably the cause of negative attitudes and results".

A more basic concern of some educators is that SC does not involve prewriting activities—figuring out what to write about. But, as explained in the next chapter, this is not a true problem in most real situations, that is, those occurring outside of English classes. When consumers write complaint letters, or when engineers write technical reports, they generally have ideas they want to write about and simply need skills to organize and express those ideas.

The most vehement argument against SC comes from some proponents of the "process approach" (discussed in the next chapter) who claim that having students write from their own emotions is the only way to teach writing, and that SC does not do this. Elbow exhorts:

> In sentence combining, the student is not engaged in figuring out what she wants to say or saying what is on her mind. And because it provides prepackaged words and ready-made thoughts, sentence combining reinforces the push-button, fast-food expectations of our culture. As a result the student is not saying anything to anyone: The results of her work are more often "answers" given to the teacher for correction—not "writing" given to readers for reactions.

With catchy, emotionally toned terms—such as "ready-made thoughts" and "fast-food expectations"—Elbow makes a convincing case. However, the propaganda ploy of using loaded language lends leverage but not clarity to language usage in the science of language learning. American education needs pedagogies founded on perceptive not just persuasive arguments. Elbow publishes widely and has been influential in retarding the acceptance of SC. The above quotation is from a paper he wrote in the 1985 publication *Sentence Combining: A Rhetorical Perspective*. So let's examine the quotation on its own terms.

First, SC does not just provide "prepackaged words." The main goal of SC is to show students how they can *repackage* words so that they have many packaging options for sending their own thoughts to readers.

Second, the fact that SC presents "ready-made thoughts" is one of its strengths: Experienced writing teachers know that "finding something to write about" is a common problem encountered with many students when the major method of trying to teach writing skills in a class is to assign papers. Cooper observes that SC provides a student "the content of the sentences so that this attention can remain focused on the *structural* aspects of the problem."

Third, exactly what Elbow means by "reinforces the push-button, fast-food expectations of our culture" is not clear in this context, but he seems to be saying that SC fits the needs and expectations of modern students. If Elbow feels he has a legitimate argument with modern American culture, he can debate this in newspaper editorials, psychology classes, or coffee houses. If he doesn't like push buttons, he can walk stairs instead of using elevators. If he doesn't like fast food, he can picket McDonald's. But his personal philosophy on lifestyle cannot stand in the way of improving writing skills for students of today's world.

Finally, two phrases which Elbow places in opposition in his last sentence do not represent opposites. " 'Answers' given to the teacher for correction is a form of " 'writing' given to readers for reactions." Elbow implies that the latter is more effective. With the former, he claims, the student "is not saying anything to anyone." The conclusion is based on Elbow's opinion that for skills to improve, writing practice must confine itself to topics of deep personal meaning addressed to nonteacher audiences.

The opinion that writing instruction must focus on helping a student uncover his or her deeper feelings is expressed in the beginning of Elbow's quotation when he criticizes SC because "the student is not engaged in figuring out what she wants to say or saying what is on her mind." But this is no more than an opinion and is contradicted by the experiences of many classroom English teachers. With most students, clear, effective learning tasks, leading to stronger language skills, evoke more serious effort than a vague assignment to write about something emotionally troubling. A study by Emig entitled *The Composing Processes of Twelfth Graders* shows that many students, especially teenage males, do not respond well to demands for the expression of private, personal feelings.

That teachers can be an audience evoking serious effort in learning objective skills is seen in athletics and other learning situations. Punters practice kicking and pitchers practice throwing endlessly yet productively only for the eyes of their coaches—their teachers. Athletes, certainly new pilots, and similarly writers, can improve their skills by practicing under the guidance of good teachers prior to performing before a nonteacher audience. Elbow's position will be back on the table for further discussion in the next chapter.

Another reservation about using SC is that it may not develop skill in organizing an entire paper. With *open* SC exercises, such as the "Hypnotism" paragraph shown earlier or the full-length essay shown later in Chapter 9, this reservation does not apply. Students are presented some sentences with main ideas and others with supporting details. They try various ways of organizing the information, and then the class discusses the strong and weak points of different arrangements.

Moreover, there is reason to believe that even cued SC leads to stronger organizing skills. Studies indicate that it improves the overall quality of student papers. Additional research is needed, but it may be that students who are facile in writing sentences can give more attention to overall organization. Based on his studies, Gebhardt suggests that SC helps students "to handle the simultaneous demands of producing, reading, judging, and modifying words."

Research also suggests that SC improves verbal reasoning ability— the ability to analyze, interpret, and relate a number of ideas— which underlies the capacity for organizing a paper. Gebhardt says SC "seems to help students learn skills and habits of abstracting and generalizing, of isolating meaning in kernels, deducing logical connections between kernels, and of compressing and blending meaning and logic from several kernels into a more compact unit with the same meaning." Just how powerful SC can be when used extensively from elementary to senior high school, rather than for just the limited time characterizing most research studies and current programs, can only be imagined.

Finally comes the concern that SC can be boring. Based on a review of many studies, however, the Hillocks survey states, "students enjoy sentence combining." Kerek, Daider, Morenberg, in an article entitled "Sentence Combining and College Composition" explain at least part of the reason for this: "Sentence combining instruction helps build confidence because it is positive in approach, it emphasizes the learning of new skills rather than the avoidance of old errors, and it subordinates every other course consideration to students' writing. After a semester of sentence combining, students usually feel better about their writing." And Mellon remarks: "I have yet to hear reports of student boredom in connection with sentence combining, and when I do I'm reasonably certain the cause will be *teacher* apathy." Once the full power of SC is recognized, textbook writers and educational researchers will devote more time and effort to developing materials that are interesting and appealing to the students for whom the exercises are intended, making the exercises even more enjoyable.

Much research is still needed comparing different SC formats and exploring how SC can be integrated with other forms of writing instruction, particularly the inquiry method described in Chapter 7 and text reconstruction covered in Chapter 4. Nevertheless, the section on SC in the most recent NCTE survey concludes:

> Even with so many questions left unanswered one is tempted to agree with Charles Cooper (1975) that "no other single teaching approach has

ever consistently been shown to have a beneficial effect on syntactic maturity and writing quality."

And the enthusiasm shown by Mellon in 1979 still seems fully appropriate: "Sentence combining produces no negative effects and works better than most of the activities in current composition teaching . . . the best advice I can give teachers today, relative to sentence combining, is—Do it! "

CHAPTER 4

The Writing Process:
Product of the Learning-to-Write
Process

A method for teaching writing called the "process approach" is on the increase in many school districts. Supporters of the method are admirably enthusiastic. They have publicized it widely through articles in professional journals and worked diligently to stamp out the use of other methods such as sentence combining which they call "unnatural writing" or "mechanistic."

However, there are signs that the process approach may look better in professional articles than in practice. Recent studies show it is not particularly effective in typical school settings. Reviewing the research lets educators and consumers of education understand what the "process approach" is and why it does not work well with many students.

The growing use of the process approach is reflected by this statement in *The Writing Report Card,* the report from the National Assessment of Educational Progress on our students' writing skills:

> . . . The emphasis in writing instruction moved from the final product to the process—planning, drafting, revising, and editing. As a result, school districts across the country have begun to institute process-oriented approaches to writing instruction.

But *The Writing Report Card* is not able to give the process approach a high grade:

> Some students did report extensive exposure to process-oriented writing activities, yet the achievement of these students was not consistently

higher or lower than the achievement of those who did not receive such
instruction. At all three grade levels assessed, students who said their
teachers regularly encouraged process-related activities wrote about as
well as students who said their teachers did not.

What exactly is this approach that "school districts across the country have begun to institute" without noticeable benefits, certainly not
matching those from sentence combining, which has tallied good results but less publicity?

Professional writers sometimes think about a piece for a while and
rewrite several drafts before submitting it for publication. This process
suggested to a group of educators that having students go through a
similar "process" would improve their writing skills. The writing process, they say, has four steps which students should follow in learning
to write. The assumption is that if students follow these steps—which
represent a rough overview of how good writers sometimes compose
and improve a paper—their skills will improve:

1. Prewrite: Think about the paper, get ideas, make notes, decide how
   to start.
2. Write a first draft.
3. Revise: Look for ways to improve the first draft.
4. Write the final draft.

There is one minor theoretical flaw in this four-step model of the
writing process: It does not even remotely represent the real-life writing process, either regarding the motivation for writing or the detailed
activities of writing. This is not a major flaw. The process approach
would still be a great idea if it were a better mousetrap, metaphorically
speaking, if it taught students to write. Let's first examine the major
flaw—why it isn't very effective in improving writing skills. Then we'll
return to the minor theoretical flaw.

The four-step model is the framework for the process approach
described neatly in professional papers and many recent English textbooks. But when you try to apply the approach, you come to the first
small problem.

Students are advised to use the first step in starting a paper, but
what paper? What should it be about? Which topic should students
write on?

The sincere student complaint, "I don't know what to write about,"
is familiar to all English teachers. The textbook *Writing with a Purpose*
admits to pupils that, "Many student writers complain that their biggest
problem is finding a subject." The Instructor's Guide warns teachers

that "The advice to 'write from what you know or what you care to learn' is often difficult for students to follow". One procedure it suggests is to "ask students to list all the subjects about which they have some expertise".

As an alternative, students may be given broad writing topics such as these:

In 300 words write about an exciting experience.

In 300 words describe and explain any changes you would like to see in schools.

Try to think of ideas for a paper on one of these topics. Most people find it takes time trying to pin down enough material to write 300 words. Typical responses from students are "I can't think of a really exciting experience that I can write about in school." "I could write about changes . . . Let me think . . . I have to write a whole 300 words? . . . I know some changes, but I don't know if I could write 300 words about them.

Because of such student difficulties, some theorists assert that each student should pick his own topic, one that is personally meaningful to him. A prominent writer in the field, Murray, explains:

The student finds his own subject. It is not the job of the teacher to legislate the student's truth. It is the responsibility of the student to explore his own world with his own language, to discover his own meaning.

Students are told that writing is a "process of discovery." Through writing, they will "discover what they have to say" and "what they really believe"—they will "construct personal meaning." In *Rhetoric and Composition*, Kelly explains, "the content of composition is the writer—the self that is revealed, thoughtfully and feelingly, in our own language, with our own voice". Emig, in a report we will review shortly, maintains that the expression of feelings is a more important form of communication than content-oriented academic writing, and that it should be encouraged more strongly by schools.

However, students are often reticent about exposing deep feelings to outsiders because true desires and reactions may be embarrassing or uninteresting. Teachers assure students that their papers do not have to be amusing or clever, just truthful. But all know that both teachers and students prefer humorous, thrilling, or surprising papers rather than dull, boring, or socially awkward ones, creating extra pressures and problems in picking a topic and generating ideas. To be successful in this social activity before the teacher, and, if papers are read aloud, peers of both gender, the student must be an entertaining writer. *Writing With a Purpose* reminds students that

> ... readers want writing that tells them something interesting or important, and they are put off by writing that is tedious or trivial. It is this wider audience that you ... must consider as you work through the writing process.

A student explained his feelings this way: "Finding something to write about is like trying to make conversation with a stranger on an elevator. You want to say something, but you don't know what to say."

Many procedures have been devised to help students think of ideas. Known collectively as *invention strategies* because they are intended to help *invent* substance for a paper, they include listing, clustering, freewriting, and journal entries.

Listing consists of writing a topic heading or title at the top of a page and then spending five or ten minutes jotting down every idea that comes to mind on the topic.

In clustering, the topic is written in a circle in the center of a page, and related associations are written as branches stretching out with twigs of details for constructing a nest of ideas. When ideas for one branch are exhausted, the writer returns to the center and begins creating another, as shown in this Figure 2.

Freewriting is another form of getting onto paper all ideas even remotely related to a topic, without trying to arrange or evaluate them. Freewriting differs from listing by using connected discourse rather than syntactically unconnected phrases and scribbles of thought. But in contrast to standard prose, freewriting is stream of consciousness outside the rhetorical and grammatical harness.

Keeping a journal as an invention strategy asks students to write perhaps 100 words in a notebook on events and ideas occurring during each day. Students are encouraged to do more than just maintain a log of events but to include feelings, reminiscences, associations, and especially ideas, examples, and phrases that might be used in a paper.

Besides these strategies and several others, some teachers have students meet in pairs or small groups to brainstorm for ideas and discuss topics for a paper.

There are two problems with all invention strategies. First, none works well. Finding things to write about remains a difficulty for many students and therefore a hindrance in using the process approach. The desperateness of the situation is seen in this example of the

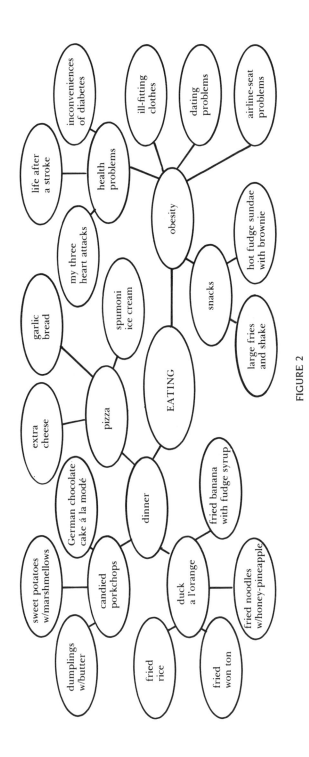

FIGURE 2

instruction teachers commonly give students to continue writing when nothing more comes to mind (from *Integrated Skills Reinforcement*):

> *Timed Writing*
>   If your topic for this paper is *education* and you don't know where to begin, for ten minutes try writing nonstop everything that comes into your mind when you hear the word education. Keep writing, even if you have to keep stating, "I don't know what to write.

The second problem with invention strategies is that they all take time away from actually learning to write. The more elaborate strategies take more time. While students are trying to think of ideas, they are not learning the writing skills and knowledge (openings, phrase formats, sentence patterns, paragraph transitions) they need in order to express and convey their ideas.

There was a hope that some of the invention strategies would themselves build writing skills. It was suggested that freewriting and keeping a journal would improve writing ability. Unfortunately, the most recent NCTE research survey reports that freewriting and keeping journals have only modest benefits for writing skills. Of all the instruction methods examined, the only one less useful than freewriting is grammar, which is totally worthless:

> Free writing asks students to write freely about whatever interests or concerns them. As a major instructional technique, free writing is more effective than teaching grammar in raising the quality of student writing. However, it is less effective than any other focus of instruction examined. Even when examined in conjunction with other features of the "process" approach model of teaching writing (writing for peers, feedback from peers, revision, and so forth), these treatments are only about two-thirds as effective as the average experimental treatment.
>   The practice of building more complex sentences from simpler ones has been shown to be effective in a large number of experimental studies. This research shows sentence combining, on the average, to be more than twice as effective as free writing as a means of enhancing the quality of student writing.

Freewriting fails, apparently, because when students write for themselves, they are not getting instruction and guidance for improvement. This is the problem plaguing the entire process approach—lack of models and feedback.

The assumption is sometimes made that since students can speak, they can learn to write just by writing. Oral language, however, differs from standard written English. Here is something a person might say:

> last night I had to get the carburetor fixed—darn car quit running on
> the way to the movie—we were right in the middle of traffic on Broadway

Oral language does not have capital letters or periods, and ideas are
often strung along rather than connected with subordinators and
coordinators. Students can learn various acceptable ways for expressing the same ideas in writing:

> Last night I had to get the carburetor fixed. The car quit running on
> the way to the movie, right in the middle of Broadway traffic.

> Last night I had to get the carburetor fixed because on the way to the
> movie, right in the middle of Broadway traffic, the car quit running.

> Because the car quit running in Broadway traffic on the way to the
> movie last night, I had to get the carburetor fixed.

> To get the car running again last night after it stopped in the middle of
> Broadway traffic on the way to the movie, I had to have the carburetor
> repaired.

Such sentence patterns and options are learned most efficiently
through direct instruction and modeling—as in sentence combining
and text reconstruction—not through working alone without examples or a coach. The NCTE survey of writing instruction drew this
conclusion: "we . . . cannot expect students to teach themselves how
to write effectively simply by writing whatever they wish for varied
groups of their peers".

Perhaps the biggest problem of invention strategies for most students is that they are needed at all. Finding something to write about
is often an artificial problem created by certain forms of writing instruction such as the process approach. In real life, situations give rise
to ideas which need to be conveyed, and only then does one decide to
write. You don't decide out-of-the-blue to write—and then have to
figure out to whom and about what.

You might receive a mail-order shirt that is the wrong size or color
and return it with a letter explaining the error and necessary correction. At a great vacation spot you might write a vivid letter home to
friends, so they will come along next year. Letters you write, ranging
from invitations letters to business memos, are generally to a particular
person for a specific purpose.

The same is true for real-life reports and papers. Whether you
write chemistry reports, business reports, history papers, psychology
papers, economic essays, or technical reports, you have ideas to convey
and you need communication skills.

In the following journal entry note that writer Eric Hoffer says the ideas for his article have "been worked out long ago," so he does not have to sit and think of things to write about:

> May 11
> The article on man and nature which I am writing for the *Saturday Evening Post* is coming along fine. Almost every idea in the train of thought has been worked out long ago. What I have to do is dovetail them more or less smoothly.

In classroom applications of the process approach, however, students must first take time inventing a topic before beginning to write and practice skills.

Once students choose a topic, they proceed to the second step in the process approach and face its second flaw. Students are told to write a first draft on a paper. But how? How should it start and what form should it take? Students are not taught language usage, sentence patterns, or models for developing ideas. They are not taught how to write the first draft.

Most skills are learned best through instruction and demonstration by an expert, followed by practice, preferably with frequent feedback and guidance from the expert. If you can afford private lessons to learn golf, the instructor demonstrates step-by-step how to hold the club, aim, swing, and follow-through. Watching golf pros is useful, but having a pro guide you through all the movements is better. The process approach makes no explicit provision for demonstration or guidance in teaching students to write. Shaw, Director of the John S. Knight Writing Program at Cornell, comments:

> Teachers interested in the writing process may turn their classes into writing workshops. . . . In at least one influential model, this workshop atmosphere follows from the belief that students already know how to write, that writing is based on innate competence for expression.

Both Achilles' heels of the process approach—inadequate modeling and paucity of feedback—intrude again in the third step: revising to improve a paper.

How can a student revise a paper without a knowledge base of writing patterns for recasting sentences, expressing ideas, and showing relationships? Studies show that when students are asked to read and improve their own papers, their changes consist primarily of correcting spelling and grammar errors. They seldom reword or combine sentences, rearrange material, or rewrite sections or paragraphs.

The process approach is based on a non sequitur. Because a good writer improves a paper by making revisions, it assumes that if students are told to revise, their skills will improve. A good writer has a collection of experiences and tricks that he or she draws on in improving a paper. A weak writer does not.

According to *The Writing Report Card,* the quality of teacher feedback is a powerful variable in the effectiveness of writing classes. But teacher feedback takes time. Suppose a teacher reads the first drafts from all of his or her students. If there are 120 students and the teachers spends 7½ minutes reading and writing comments on each paper, this comes to 15 hours—15 hours beyond full-time preparation and teaching.

Quick feedback (overnight turnover) is best—which means marking for hours in the evening. Furthermore, studies show that many students hardly glance at comments on papers. They benefit most if comments are not just written on their papers but explained in a one-to-one conference giving detailed guidance or specific assignments for improving particular weaknesses. In reality, this expands beyond feasibility the time required for the feedback needed by many students to improve their writing with the process approach. Optimistically, some teachers do try to schedule short, individual conferences with students. But add to this another fifteen hours for grading the revised, final papers, and the teacher has a work week of over 70 hours. Teachers who really try to teach writing this way are very tired at the end of the school year, and many burn out.

In attempting to deal with this, the process approach generally has students meet in pairs or small groups to read aloud or exchange papers, giving and getting suggestions for improvement. The process approach takes the following form when group meetings are included:

1. Prewrite: Think about the paper, use invention strategies, meet in groups to get ideas, make notes, decide how to start.
2. Write a first draft.
3. Meet in groups to read aloud or exchange papers and get suggestions for revision.
4. Write the final draft.
5. Proofread: Correct spelling, punctuation, and other mechanical errors.

Some teachers have reported the successful use of peer discussion for revision. But many find that in their classes it exemplifies the phrase "the blind leading the blind." The same lack of knowledge which prevents students from writing well and revising their own papers prevents them from giving good feedback to others. Also, they tend to be too generous with compliments, not wanting to hurt each other's feelings with criticism.

In her first-semester junior college writing classes, Linden asked students to find one point to praise in each paper and to make one suggestion for improvement. But the students confined their suggestions mainly to correcting mechanical errors, particularly in spelling and capitalization. In their eyes no paper was so thin in content or details that they passed judgment on a classmate to go back and do more writing. They seemed either undisturbed or too kind to note when the organization of a paper was totally chaotic. Over many years of teaching high school and college English, Linden tried peer revision groups with about a dozen classes, but it worked well only once, in an advanced second-semester college class. It never succeeded with typical high school or freshmen college students, leaving Linden herself to evaluate and make comments on first drafts, hold one-to-one conferences, and grade final papers—the conscientious English teacher's 70-hour work week.

A report by Emig entitled *The Composing Processes of Twelfth Graders* casts a revealing light on the entire revision stage of the process model. Emig studied the writing processes of high school students by interviewing them and observing them as they wrote. Several of the students had been identified as strong writers by their teachers and had won writing awards. Emig found that these strong students write good first drafts of papers and then stop, without going back and doing much revising. When asked about revision, they say they usually do not bother revising if their papers are good enough. They regard revising as a tedious punishment for students who make too many errors. Because Emig believes in the four-stage process approach, she recommends that all students should be taught to revise. In the same report, she also asserts that many English teachers are not well-prepared to teach writing. Poor instruction, she says, is "partially attributable to teacher illiteracy. . . . More crucial, many teachers of composition, at least below the college level, themselves do not write." While these are personal opinions, not research findings, Emig helped organize a series of continuing workshops to upgrade English teachers' competence—by teaching them the process approach.

Emig's finding that good students often do not revise pinpoints another troublesome flaw in the four-stage writing approach, namely that the four stages distort through oversimplification the real writing process.

Writing and rewriting are constantly intertwined. They are not separate stages. In writing, you may start to formulate a sentence in one form but before you begin hitting the keyboard, recast it into another form. Already you have revised. Then you type three sentences, read them over, and see how the first and second can be combined. After writing several paragraphs, and again at the end of the page, you may reread and find things to revise. Writers seldom write a first draft without looking back, then shift into stage 2 and reread the entire draft for things to modify, then shift into stage 3 and go straight through making all the modifications.

Quite often, after completing a first draft—and knowing all the thought and revision that went into it it—a writer has no intention of doing any more revising. He or she rereads the draft solely because he or she knows from experience there are always spelling and typing errors to correct. Sometimes the writer finds a sentence to recast here, an idea to extend there, and spends two more full days with innumerable minor and major revisions. But other times he or she is lucky, corrects two spelling errors, adds a comma, and is done.

Revising can be hard, time-consuming work. Often a first draft is good enough. A writer may only bother doing substantial revising if there is a particular interest in making a point with some audience. Rereading a paper with a strong interest in its effectiveness — picturing the reactions, background, and biases of the audience — one may see ways to improve the presentation of ideas. But students seldom have such a strong motivation for polishing papers in English classes.

Some textbooks spend many paragraphs admonishing students to write for this or that particular audience with diligence and craftsmanship, taking ownership of their papers as important publishable documents. But expecting them to be so strongly motivated by a "pretend" situation that they undertake taxing cognitive labor to revise an already satisfactory written communication is like expecting them to work for a nice present from Santa Claus.

That a separate revision stage is not an indispensable part of all good writing is seen again in these observations from the *New York Times Book Review* of a novel team-written by students in Ken Kesey's creative writing class:

> Since "Caverns" aims to be both an intriguing tale and a revolutionary model for the teaching of creative writing, it might be worthwhile to explore the ways in which Mr. Kesey's methods work or fail to work. Most successful writers value the advice and suggestions of colleagues and editors, and Mr. Kesey's emphasis on a spirit of friendly collaboration is likely to help beginning writers learn how to accept or reject criticism. The focus, however, of Mr. Kesey's class is clearly on writing, not revision. There is much to be said for his insistence that students be

required to write for a set period of time and then immediately read their work. Apparently, such a technique does not permit either writer's block or the endless revising of each passage, problems that can easily plague novice writers.

Emig's finding that strong students possess skills which allow them to write a good first draft without a separate revision stage suggests that English classes need a pedagogy for effectively teaching such strong skills to more students in today's schools. Then students can use these skills to revise when they have a reason to.

Familiarizing students with the writing process, namely that experienced writers often take appreciable time getting ideas, that new ideas and insights may occur as they write, and that they often revise and rewrite extensively, can be worthwhile. Students can be encouraged to use these aids in writing original papers after doing text reconstruction exercises described in the next chapter. Also, in advanced content courses—literature, history, chemistry—students meeting in groups to discuss first drafts of papers and reports might provide useful feedback in clarifying concepts, relationships, or operations. They might learn to write more clearly, teach each other report formats and course content, and come to appreciate the usefulness of revision.

But making the writing process the main focus for instruction in English classes has not been successful. The process approach highlights steps writers sometimes use to write and polish a paper, although the steps are generally blurred and intermingled. But these steps have not been a faithful guide for improving the skills of students. The steps may roughly represent the writing process, but they do not represent the best learning-to-write process. They are perhaps steps for writing a paper—but not for teaching writing ability. The NCTE survey of writing instruction concludes:

> The research on the composing process provides little evidence to suggest that free writing as a main focus in the natural process mode of instruction will be effective. While Graves and his colleagues argue in favor of letting children choose their own topics, write what they want, submit it to peer review, and then revise, some of the actual evidence presented is negative, and some suggests that their subjects' writing is not so free as it might be.

Elsewhere, Graves observes:

> Teachers of English should, of course, help their young charges with problems of conceptualization and discovery, but they cannot stop there. They must go on to a task which is not as glamorous yet just as important,

for those beginners must learn how to become consummate craftsmen of the language.

Graves mentions three concern of English teachers—discovery, conceptualization, and craftsmanship. Discovery can be left as the last priority: People generally write because they have information they want to convey—facts, explanations, complaints, instructions, compliments. They don't need to "discover" a subject to write about. They need conceptualization skills—the ability to verbalize and organize their ideas—and craftsmanship.

Viewing conceptualization as verbalization and organization shows its close kinship to craftsmanship and explains why the entire group of skills underlying both conceptualization and craftsmanship is strengthened through the same pair of instructional methods—sentence combining and a technique developed by professional writers for improving their own skills, text reconstruction, the subject of the next chapter.

CHAPTER 5

Text Reconstruction: Flying By Imitation

Benjamin Franklin, one of America's first noteworthy writers, describes in his autobiography a method he used to improve his writing skill. As a youth he worked in his brother's print shop where articles by many fine writers were published. When he admired an essay, he wrote several words from each sentence. These he calls "short hints of the sentiment in each sentence." Next he mixed the hints into random order and set them aside.

Several weeks later Franklin tried to arrange the hints into their original order to recreate the logical organization of the essay. He says, "This was to teach me method in the arrangement of thoughts." Then the future author of *Poor Richard's Almanac* attempted to write each sentence from just the hints, checking back to the original and noting any deviations, trying to master the vocabulary, sentence structure, and style of the writer.

Jack London used a similar procedure of analyzing and reconstructing selections of admired prose. According to the *New York Times Book Review* Jack London, who wrote *The Sea Wolf* and is the most widely read American author in the world, was raised penniless and worked at many hard, low-paying jobs before embarking on a literary career. When in his mid-twenties he decided to become a professional writer, he "analyzed the stories he liked, or copied them out by hand to learn how they were put together, and wrote his own pieces with their example in mind."

A variation of Franklin's text reconstruction (TRC) is used in the workbook *Analytical Writing and Thinking*. The authors wrote sample papers and then jumbled the sentences. Students number the senten-

Instructions: Read all the sentences. Decide which should come first and number it 1. Then decide which should come second and number it 2. Continue numbering the remaining sentences this way.

___ Therefore when nineteen-year-old Michael Grubbs became this year's queen, it shocked no one.

___ One year its queen was a dog and another year a refrigerator.

___ Rice University has had some unusual homecoming queens in the past.

___ So Michael has agreed to give up his title and escort his runner-up, Nancy Jones, to the festivities.

___ But Cotton Bowl rules prohibit a man from being a princess in the parade.

Check your numbers with a neighbor if possible. Where you disagree, explain to each other why you arranged the sentences as you did.

Next, copy the sentences in the order you numbered them on a separate sheet of paper. Copying sentences can be especially helpful for improving writing skills if done as Ben Franklin did—from memory. Do not just copy word-for-word. For each sentence, follow these steps:

1. Read as many words as you believe you can write correctly from memory (usually five to ten words).
2. Write those words from memory, including all capitals and punctuation marks.
3. Check back to the original sentence and correct any errors you made.
4. Read the next groups of words and repeat the steps.

Generally you will be able to read, memorize, and correctly write between five and ten words. Sometimes you may be able to remember an entire simple sentence correctly. But with a large, difficult-to-spell word, you may try to write only that one word correctly from memory.

Writing from memory is a powerful technique for learning the spelling, grammar, punctuation, and word patterns used in standard written English.

FIGURE 3

ces in what they consider the best order. Then they compare arrangements and discuss differences with other students, pinpointing the information and logic they employ. Finally, they write the sentences in the order numbered.

Figure 3 shows a sample exercise along with the instructions from the workbook.

Through arranging sentences and discussing their rationale, students gradually learn to read more accurately: They learn to focus on grasping the full meaning of each sentence so that logical relationships between sentences can be understood.

Students also learn to recognize and use coherence and cohesion devices employed by effective writers. They see the cues, transition words—such as "so," "but," and "therefore"—and relationship patterns that enable them to order the sentences. Gradually they see how these cues can be used in their own writing.

What Franklin called "method in the arrangement of thoughts" is more commonly known as logical organization, a major area of weakness in student papers. One of the most common forms of logical organization found in writing is generalization supported by specific details. Many high school graduates have not learned the necessary thinking skills to work from the general to the specific, observes Morton, which not only makes them poor writers but also leaves them unable to master study skills such as outlining and note-taking.

Here is a TRC exercise from *Analyze, Organize, Write* modeling general-specific organization for students.

SET 4. THE COMPANY NEEDS A NEW TRUCK

When you recommend an expensive purchase like buying a new truck, you need convincing reasons with specific facts to win your case. The following sentences can be arranged to make a well-supported argument for a new truck.

Exercise 1. Number the sentences within each paragraph to form the best logical order.

I

_____ Nevertheless, we should buy a new truck because the old truck is unreliable, obtaining parts for it is difficult, and the greater economy of a new truck would help repay the purchase price.

_____ It is true that new trucks are expensive and the company's budget is tight.

II

_____ Worst yet, last Friday it quit running on the expressway and had to be towed to a garage.

_____ Three times last month deliveries to customers were late because the truck would not start.

_____ The company is sure to lose business if this continues.

_____ The old truck is constantly breaking down.

III

_____ This means they have to special-order the parts, which usually takes several hours and once took 2 days.

_____ Another problem is getting replacement parts.

_____ Because of its age, most repair shops don't carry the hoses, belts, mufflers, or other parts it requires.

IV

_____ Our old clunker only gets about 12 miles per gallon on the highway and less in the city.

_____ There are not only the savings on repair costs, but we can choose a truck that gets much better gas mileage.

_____ Looking at the brighter side, a new truck would eventually pay for itself.

_____ All things considered, buying a new truck makes a lot of sense.

_____ Some of the newer models average as much as 30 or 40 miles per gallon.

Exercise 2. Write the sentences in the order you numbered them to form a short paper that expresses an opinion that a certain action should be taken, then supports that opinion with three specific reasons (including examples).

In this paper, students learn to organize ideas in the logical pattern of main idea supported by topic sentences, these in turn supported by specific content. The main idea of the first paragraph guides readers to the topic sentences of the three body paragraphs. Once students locate the topic sentence for each paragraph, they must think their way through the arrangement of the support sentences, and also select the most appropriate ending sentence.

This paper is a variation of what is called _the five-paragraph theme,_ consisting of an opening paragraph that states the main idea and three pieces of evidence supporting it; three body paragraphs, each expanding on one piece of supporting evidence; and a conclusion paragraph summarizing it all. This paper, being simple, lacks a conclusion paragraph and just ends with the last sentence of the fourth paragraph.

The next TRC illustrates another variation of the five-paragraph theme. This one does have all five paragraphs, but the first does not list the three pieces of supporting evidence covered in the middle three paragraphs. Instead, it explains and expands on the main idea.

Instructions: Here is a typical writing test topic.

There are many common sayings like "Do not count your chickens before they hatch." Pick any common saying and analyze it by explaining what it means and giving examples supporting or contradicting it.

Number the sentences within each paragraph in the best order to form a paper on this topic.

Lightning and Larcenists Strike Twice

Introduction

_____ This saying claims that misfortune is fair and does not haunt one location or person.

_____ A saying I hear periodically is "Lightning never strikes in the same place twice."

_____ Unfortunately, this sweet thought is often wrong.

_____ It is used to console tragedy-stricken people by telling them disaster won't strike again: they are through the worst, and things are going to improve.

Body Paragraph

_____ So lightning—or at least car thieves—will probably strike here again.

_____ For example, I have a friend whose customized Corvette has been stolen three times.

_____ Worse yet, the police told him there is a car-theft ring in our city which specializes in unique sports cars.

_____ He spent over $1500 trying every available anti-theft device, but none worked.

Body Paragraph

_____ In fact, last summer a pick-up truck scored six points for totally demolishing it while trying to avoid a football that got away from some youngsters.

_____ At least once every winter when there is ice on the street a car knocks it over.

_____ Another example is a traffic light on a safety island near school.

Body Paragraph

_____ He usually did not have the bus fare to burglarize another neighborhood.

_____ The frequency that the traffic light gets hit is low compared to the frequency the 7-11 in my neighborhood gets hit by armed robbers.

_____ Two weeks ago the police finally captured a junkie who had robbed the store three times in the last year.

Conclusion

_____ All and all, I think the saying should be changed to, "Lightning often strikes twice—even hundreds of times—in the same place, so steer clear of such places."

_____ In fact, the Empire State Building, a huge lightning rod in the center of Manhattan, gets struck by over one hundred bolts of volts a year.

_____ There are many other examples of bad fortune being a regular visitor to some place or person.

Exercise 2. Check your numbers with a neighbor. If your answers differ, explain why you arranged the sentences the way you did.

Exercise 3. Write the sentences in the order you numbered them. Write from memory as much as possible.

Some English educators feel the five-paragraph theme has been overemphasized, since much real-life writing does not take that form; we will show a TRC exercise later which teaches students to use the form flexibly. However, TRC is not limited to the five-paragraph form. Here is a TRC exercise giving students a model for writing a thumbnail description of a person.

Thumbnail Description of a Person

Exercise 1. Number the sentences to describe a man in the following order: overall body (size, type), face, grooming (hair, clothes), general impression.

_____ His hair was fashionably cut, falling just above his collar in the back.

_____ His blue suit and grey-patterned tie with matching handkerchief had been carefully chosen at a fine men's shop.

_____ The young, new manager, was tall and athletic-looking, with broad shoulders, a trim waist, and firm muscles filling out his clothing.

_____ He was the picture of confidence and success.

_____ He had high cheekbones, a strong jaw, and eyes that seemed to glow with vitality.

Exercise 2. Write the sentences in the order you numbered them.

Exercise 3. With all material from exercises 1 and 2 put away, write a
brief description of a friend, relative, or imaginary person
in terms of body type, face, grooming, general impression,
and any other characteristics you consider important.

This exercise models a systematic description of a person. When students write their own papers, their personalities push through, bending and stretching the model with extra attention to details that interest them. A student with a sense of humor may exaggerate characteristics to caricature someone. A student sensitive to people's eyes and facial expressions will naturally write more about them.

Earlier we described forms of TRC used by Franklin and London in perfecting their craft. Is TRC also effective with the many weak and average students in modern schools? Improvements produced by TRC in the content and organization of papers from community college basic writing students are reflected by the following *before* and *after* paragraphs from three representative students.

Student A: Paragraph Written Before TRC
I have had this bad habit of smoking for twenty years. An have tried to stop for twenty years, but have not tried very hard. But I still keep trying. Once I quit for—Eleven month an I gain thirty lbs. so I used this weight gain as a weak excuse to start smoking again.

Five weeks later: Definition Paragraph
Pollution is the unnecessary destruction of health, nature, land, air, water, and even the future which is a crime against humanity. Here is something that happened to me to show this meaning: The first time that I was aware of pollution, I was about twelve years old and hunting plain along the Illinois River as I walked accross an area that a roof-company had pumped their waste it looked like a giant colored parking lot covering a area of the plain and totaly destroying a beautiful pond which I had just fished 3 months before. On close inspection of the pond I could see that it was filled with tar, oil, waste and the smell was so bad you could hardly stand it. This was a form of pollution you could see and smell.

The richer development through specific details shown in the second paper comes from the constant practice in the arrangement of content into general-specific patterns provided by text reconstruction. The second paper also shows much-improved sentence structure with complex sentences replacing the simple and compound sentences of the first. In addition, a variety of sentence openers are used.

Here is what another student wrote before TRC when asked to

write a *paragraph* on a personal experience. His lack of "sense of paragraph" is shown by the many indented sentences.

Student B: Paragraph Assignment Before TRC
Being accused of something you did not do is an unpleasant experience.
I know at one time in our life maybe as a child you may have been accused of something that was unfair. Parents jury your wronged.
The emotion that you experience are all mix up inside you. You feet hurt, made, sad and angry all at once. You become easily sensitive to future problems.
Even went you are clear of the wrong doing you'll always remember that experience.

Twelve weeks later: Paragraph from Opinion Paper
The second improvement that Joliet needs is entertainment for teenagers in various forms. From the East Side of town the nearest movie is ten miles away at the Jefferson Street Mall. The Town and Country Bowling Lanes is also on the West Side of Joliet. And if a teenager does not own a car it would be difficult to obtain transportation. Because the buses stop running after 6:00 with no service at all on Sunday or Holiday.

The second sample demonstrates the student's ability to handle paragraph form. Also, in contrast to the generalities of the first, it is full of specific details, such as, "From the East Side of town. . . ." Further, this young man has learned to use cohesion devices: "The second improvement" and "also."
Here is the work of one more student:

Student C: Paragraph Written Before TRC
The best movie I've seen recently is "The Killing field." Why I said this movie is good. Because it was a true story of Cambodia. This movie showed how miserable all the Cambodian people during Communist took over, and talking about Cambodian translater was a good honest man with his American reporter friend, stucked with communist for 5 years and finally try to escape the country and got succeeded, how he lived in United States.

Twelve Weeks Later: From Opinion Paper
The United States is an enjoyable place to live. Having been born and raised in Cambodia and also having traveled through Europe I know the United States is the best place to live. . . . Secondly opportunity most people in this country live in the middle class of society. If you work hard you can have just about anything you want. You can study and improve your way of life and your job; therefore, increasing your income. You don't need to be a doctor or engineer to own your own home or car because with good credit you can get a loan. In Cambodia, my dad worked hard seven days a week with no time off to afford one

home, two cars, and send my brother to college. There were no such thing as loans.

Instead of the scrambled constructions marred with verb errors of the first sample, in the second this student, learning English as a second language, uses sophisticated sentences with participial phrases and prepositional phrase openers. She also uses complex sentences opening and closing with adverbial clauses and demonstrates the use of cohesion devices such as "Secondly."

All three continued to have proofreading problems and make mechanical errors (although less frequently), requiring additional work. But all three learned to organize coherent paragraphs and furnish specific details to support general statements.

In describing weak writers—estimated to be roughly 70% of America's 11th graders—*The Writing Report Card* observes that they understood "what is required in" an analytical writing assignment, but their evidence is "disorganized or unelaborated. Rather than using coherent arguments or explanations, far too many students resorted to simple lists . . ." As reflected by the above papers and those of other students, focussing on the learning-to-write process teaches students to elaborate and organize evidence, and thus prepares them for the process of writing.

TRC involves analyzing an author's ideas and copying his or her language to strengthen one's own analytical and writing skills. The TRC program at the Handy Colony for writers is described by McShane in his biography of James Jones, author of *From Here to Eternity:*

> But even before the colonists did work of their own, they were required to sit down at their typewriters and copy out lengthy passages from published novels or complete short stories. . . . The novelists whose works were chosen were selected according to the individual's needs. . . .The act of copying was also intended to make young writers find out what it is like to finish an extended piece of work. Jones himself said that one could read until his eyes are red, but only by copying word for word could one see how a writer builds up his effects. The copying was also intended to help young writers learn how to handle transitions from one scene to another. They were to learn economy of expression and become less prolix. . . . Lowney did not want her writers to imitate the writers they copied; on the contrary, she chose passages for copying that were unlike the young writer's own style in order to force him to develop other ways of expression. . . . What she hoped for was a process of osmosis from the published writer to the unpublished.

An excerpt from one of Jones' letters shows his enthusiasm for copying:

Well, the typewriters are really going mornings, as you can imagine.
We've even got the twins working, copying fairy tales. Alma is copying
Hemingway, and Bob a mixture of Hindu Yoga and Hammett and
Raymond Chandler. You would be amazed what this copying system,
which I wrote you about a long time ago, does for them. Take Willy: he
is, after about two years, at the place of technical (and mental—spiritual,
if you will) proficiency that I was at about two or three years ago, after
working at it for at least five years.

Whereas Jones learned the benefits of analytical copying at the
Handy Colony, Somerset Maugham reports in *The Summing Up* that,
"I have had to teach myself." He began copying only outstanding
words and phrases:

It was generally thought then that the Authorized Version of the Bible
was the greatest piece of prose that the English language has produced.
I read it diligently, especially the Song of Solomon, jotting down for
future use turns of phrases that struck me and making lists of unusual
or beautiful words.

Later he started TRC activities in earnest:

I studied Jeremy Taylor's *Holy Dying*. In order to assimilate his style, I
copied out passages and then tried to write them down from memory.

Unsatisfied with the book he wrote after studying Taylor and seeking
a master stylist whose writing was more to his taste, he turned to the
Augustan Period:

The prose of Swift enchanted me. I made up my mind that this was a
perfect way to write, and I started to work on him in the same way as I
had done with Jeremy Taylor. . . . As I had done before, I copied passages and then tried to write them out again from memory. I tried alter-
ing words or the order in which they were set. I found that the only possible words were those Swift had used and that the order in which he had
placed them was the only possible order. It is impeccable prose.

Regarding this experience, Maugham says, "The work I did was certainly very good for me. I began to write better."
In TRC exercises such as "Lightning and Larcenists Strike Twice,"
students are asked to copy from memory rather than letter by letter.
They are encouraged to read as many words as they think they can
write from memory, write from memory, and then check back with
the original. Copying has been used to improve writing throughout
history by writers such as Shakespeare, although it is hardly seen in

modern English classes. It is consistent with the view expressed by
Gorrell that many weak writers must learn English as a dialect or
second language. Lacking the background and habits to produce aca-
demically acceptable prose, they need to practice writing correct forms
until such forms become habitual, advise Friedmann and MacKillop.

Copying is a time-honored device in learning how to write, dating
back to the Romans. In Shakespeare's time schoolboys learned to write
in both Latin and English by extensive use of their copybooks and
commonplace books, reports Baldwin. Commonplace books are handwritten classified anthologies of copied arguments and quotations used
as source books for essays and serious pieces of writing. Thomas
Jefferson, for example, copied widely and commented on the entries
in his commonplace book.

An extraordinary program of analytical copying—copying with the
intention to understand and learn—is reported by Malcolm X. In his
autobiography he says that when he entered prison, although he was
an effective public speaker, his reading and writing skills were very
poor, a distinct hindrance in writing letters to political allies and offi-
cials on the outside. To remedy this, he recalls:

> I saw that the best thing I could do was get hold of a dictionary—to
> study, to learn some words. I was lucky enough to reason also that I should
> try to improve my penmanship. It was sad. I couldn't even write in a
> straight line. It was both ideas together that moved me to request a diction-
> ary along with some tablets and pencils from the Norfolk Prison Colony
> school.
>
> I spent two days just riffling uncertainly through the dictionary's pages.
> I'd never realized so many words existed! I didn't know *which* words I
> needed to learn. Finally, just to start some kind of action, I began copying.
>
> In my slow, painstaking, ragged handwriting, I copied into my tablet
> everything printed on that first page, down to the punctuation marks.
>
> I believe it took me a day. Then, aloud, I read back, to myself, every-
> thing I'd written on the tablet. Over and over, aloud, to myself, I read my
> own handwriting.
>
> I woke up the next morning, thinking about those words—immensely
> proud to realize that not only had I written so much at one time, but I'd
> written words that I never knew were in the world. Moreover, with a little
> effort, I also could remember what many of these words meant. I reviewed
> the words whose meanings I didn't remember. Funny thing, from the
> dictionary first page right now, that "aardvark" springs to my mind. The
> dictionary had a picture of it, a long-tailed, long-eared, burrowing African
> mammal, which lives off termites caught by sticking out its tongue as an
> anteater does for ants.
>
> I was so fascinated that I went on—I copied the dictionary's next page.

He went on to copy the entire dictionary.

Franklin's form of TRC, the combination of arranging sentences and copying them from memory, teaches students to organize ideas and then express them with the vocabulary, spelling, punctuation, and syntax of standard written English. This modeling is especially useful for students learning English as a second language, or from backgrounds with differing dialects.

Experienced teachers know it is generally more efficient to use a published workbook rather than to create original exercises and distribute handouts. Devising, typing, and reproducing them takes many hours. Handouts can be blurry when the Xerox machine is not working well. They also get lost and are thus unavailable for illustrating ideas later in class.

But for teachers, parents, and students who cannot find an appropriate workbook—who create their own TRC exercises from magazines, history textbooks, or literary pieces—some possibilities are illustrated in the next pages.

Generally, six sentences are the maximum number that can be placed in a jumbled set for students to rearrange logically. More can produce confusion unless the sentences are simple and only semijumbled. Longer paragraphs may be separated into two sets of sentences which are rejoined when the paper is written. Or some sentences in long paragraphs can be prenumbered and others presorted into roughly first and second half as shown in the next exercise.

TRC can be used to model writing of any type or format. For example, narration is considered a primary form of writing in most rhetorical theories. Here is an exercise giving students a model for narrating an exciting experience:

SET 5. RAW RAGE

narrative ✓

Can you recall and describe a series of events leading to an incident that left you shocked, injured, and forever more cautious? The following sentences can be arranged to tell such a story.

Exercise 1. Number the sentences within each paragraph so they sound best to you. You may discover more than one good arrangement for some paragraphs.

> Vocabulary
> agony: intense pain of mind or body.

anguish: intense pain, especially of mind.
confrontation: face-to-face meeting of enemies.
deter: stop, delay.
instincts: inborn drives
minor: unimportant.
momentary: lasting just a moment.
temporarily: for a short period of time.

I

_____ After almost 12 years of treating this animal as if he were a child—caring for him during his illnesses, providing him with the best of food, holding him for countless hours, and loving him as a faithful companion—he bit me as if I were a total stranger.

_____ Although it was not as serious as a disease or a life-threatening accident, it has caused me much physical pain and mental anguish.

_____ My cat bit me.

_____ Last summer I had a painful, scarring experience.

II

_____ I admit that I was not blameless in the incident.

_____ He was involved in a fight with another cat.

_____ And I had been warned many times about the consequences of interfering in such a confrontation.

_____ By the time I arrived they were fighting and rolling on a neighbor's porch like characters out of a western movie.

_____ Nevertheless, at the first howls of battle, I went to rescue him.

_____ My screams to stop were ignored; they continued to fight.

_____ Even falling from the porch onto hard concrete did not deter them for a moment.

III

_____ I followed them across the street as they chased each other under and between parked cars.

_____ Eventually they came to a momentary standoff under a red van.

_____ As I tried to coax my cat out, the other cat broke his stance and ran into the underbrush of a neighboring yard.

_____ My cat followed, but suddenly, as if bored by the whole thing, he returned to where I was standing.

_____ He purred and rubbed against my leg.

_____ Then I picked him up and headed toward home.

_____ I bent down and patted him affectionately, noting scratches on his ears and nose that would soon be scars for life.

_____ I tried to drop him, but I moved too slowly.

_____ All at once his body stiffened and a threatening growl came from deep inside his throat.

_____ Then I felt his fangs puncture my flesh and sink deeper and deeper until they struck a bone.

_____ He twisted around in my arms, and I felt his mouth close around my wrist.

IV

_____ When he finally let go, blood flowed down the front and back of my hand as it began swelling to twice its normal size.

_____ It throbbed with pain; only thoughts of the need to clean the wounds got me to my feet again.

_____ Fourteen pounds of unleashed fury hung from my wrist.

_____ I fell to my knees and slung my arm, trying to get him to release me.

V

__3__ I still could not believe that my cat had attacked me so viciously.

_____ The pain was constant, but that was minor compared to the mental agony I was suffering.

_____ For 3 days my wrist and palm were so swollen that I could not open or close my hand.

_____ Those other owners probably held the same belief, until their pets reacted to instincts temporarily blinded and out of control.

_____ I had heard horror stories about other animals attacking their owners, but I had been sure that our relationship was different, stronger.

VI

_____ Oh, I still pat him, feed him, let him sit at my feet, but I do not pick him up and hold him in my arms—not yet.

_____ Today my wrist has four puncture scars that will be there forever.

_____ Of that part I remain very fearful.

_____ The scars on our relationship are also permanent.

_____ I still love him, but I do not trust that part of his being that denied the existence of our relationship.

Exercise 2. Write the sentences in the order you numbered them to form a story about a series of events that left the writer with a lingering fear of animals.

The papers "Raw Rage" and "The Company Needs a New Truck" (presented earlier) have fairly simple sentences and vocabularies. In preparing to deal with advanced high school and college courses, students can gradually move to material with more complicated ideas and sentences, requiring more processing to fully interpret symbols and mentally reconstruct relationships. This is illustrated in the next paper, which distinguishes the connotative definition of "stepparent" from the denotative definition.

SET 4. STEPPARENT BLUES

What associations does the word stepparent bring to mind? Do you think of a mean, selfish person like Cinderella's stepmother? Here is the meaning of "stepparent" for a writer who is a stepparent.

Exercise 1. Number the sentences within each paragraph to form the best logical order.

> Vocabulary
> acquire: get, obtain.
> advocate: a person who argues for the wishes of another.
> co-conspirator: one who aids in an unlawful plan.
> connotations: feelings and associations suggested by a word.
> ego: self-pride, self-esteem.
> ogre: monster, horrible giant that eats humans.
> suspect (used as an adjective): open to suspicion.
> reminiscing: thinking or talking about the past.
> superficial: dealing only with the surface, shallow, lacking deep
>   understanding.
> tabloid: small size newspaper often with much sensationalistic
>   news and gossip.
> whims: sudden wishes or desires.

I

_____ It simply describes a stepparent as "the person who has married one's parent after the death or divorce of the other parent."

_____ Webster's gives a rather superficial definition of the word "stepparent."

_____ However, most stepparents have had experiences that give a much broader meaning to the word.

_____ This definition makes it seem easy to be a stepparent.

II

_____ But the word still sounds ugly and carries mean connotations.

_____ Today, as the divorce rate soars, the stepparent is becoming a common member of the family unit.

__3_ For centuries, stepparents have received more than their fair share of unkind press.

_____ In fact, due to these and other stories, stepmothers have become so suspect that many tales made up by children contain a "wicked stepmother" who terrorizes everyone in the fantasy.

_____ After all, wasn't it Cinderella's stepmother who almost worked the poor child to death?

_____ And wasn't Snow White's stepmother so jealous that she tried to kill the little princess?

_7_ Stepfathers haven't fared much better.

_____ Mr. Murdstone in _David Copperfield_ proved to be about as cruel as a stepfather could be.

_____ And tabloids have spread the news of stepfathers who have abused, molested, and murdered their stepchildren.

_____ In _Hamlet_, it was his stepfather who tried to murder the Danish prince.

III

_____ Now I hear protests of, "You don't know my stepmother (or stepfather)!" from some of you, and I admit you are right.

_____ Although in reality some stepparents are wicked and abusive, many more are nothing but good and kind to their stepchildren.

_____ But if the majority of you are honest, you will have to admit that your stepparent really isn't an ogre waiting for the chance to ruin your life forever.

_____ I don't know your stepparent, and he or she may be terrible.

IV

_____ And through the games of ego versus ego versus id, I have learned well the roles I am expected to play.

_____ The experiences that I've had are like a mixture of homemade sweet and sour sauce; even now I never know just what the "taste" of any situation is going to be.

_____ Putting all the fantastic tales and dictionary definitions aside, I believe I know what a stepparent really is because for 5 years I've known the burdens and the joys that accompany the title.

V

_____ I have also learned how to act at my husband's family gatherings when the <u>other</u> grandparents drop in and stay for hours reminiscing about the happy times when "the children" were married.

_____ As a stepparent I have learned to play the role of the cause for the breakup of my husband's first marriage and the disruptive effects it had on my stepchild, even though the marriage ended long before my husband and I met.

VI

_____ And early in my marriage I learned how to play the one who stayed at home when an outing suddenly became a "twosome."

__2__ Then I was expected to be the "absentee" when they could be present.

_____ Another role I learned was that of the "attendee" (my word) at school plays, dance recitals, and music extravaganzas when the real parents couldn't be there.

_____ But the most hurtful part I learned to play was how to watch my stepchild give good night kisses to everyone in the room—except me.

VII

_____ And more than once I have been a protector when tasks went undone or standards were not met.

__2__ Also, I have been the advocate when whiney whims became angry demands that soon turned to pitiful cries.

_____ Some of the sweeter times have occurred when my role required me to become a co-conspirator in helping acquire some wanted treasure, such as roller skates, a bicycle, or a computer.

_____ But these feelings lasted only until it was time for the child to visit the other parent, and he rushed off without remembering to say good-bye.

_____ During those times I said to myself, "I am the only person in the world who really understands this child."

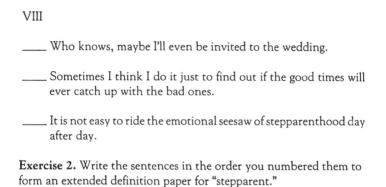

VIII

_____ Who knows, maybe I'll even be invited to the wedding.

_____ Sometimes I think I do it just to find out if the good times will ever catch up with the bad ones.

_____ It is not easy to ride the emotional seesaw of stepparenthood day after day.

Exercise 2. Write the sentences in the order you numbered them to form an extended definition paper for "stepparent."

ASSIGNING ORIGINAL PAPERS

It is not necessary to follow every TRC exercise with an assignment to students for an original paper. Students learn writing skills from the TRC exercises. Several can be presented before a paper is assigned, just as a teacher might suggest several reading selections before requiring a paper. The difference between TRC and regular reading is that TRC encourages active processing of the material, with detailed study of the content and organization—as Jones emphasized with his comment that one could read until his eyes are read, but only by copying word for word could one see how a writer builds up his effect.

Earlier we discussed "Lightning and Larcenists Strike Twice," a five-paragraph theme on a common saying. The five-paragraph theme was the quintessential writing assignment for many years in English classes. Recently some English educators have objected to its use, pointing out that most real-life pieces of writing do not fit this neat format. In her research report, Emig rechristens it the "Fifty-Star Theme" to satirize its wide usage in schools. But many teachers still feel it makes an effective exercise by providing a framework for students who are not accustomed to organizing their ideas in writing.

Rather than totally banish the five-paragraph theme, we can teach students to use it flexibly and see it as just one format for supporting a generalizations with sufficient, convincing details. In *Analytical Writing and Thinking*, after students reconstruct "Lightning and Larcenists . . ." they do another TRC with instructions explaining that they can use a different format if it is more appropriate for the paper they write and the experiences they highlight.

Illustration

✓

Instructions: The last paper you wrote employs three examples to disprove the saying "Lightning never strikes twice." Sometimes it is unnecessary to use several examples to illustrate a point. One example rich with details can present a convincing picture for your readers, as you will see in the next paper.

Exercise 1. Number the sentences within each paragraph in the best order.

Do Not Judge a Lady by Her Bags

Introduction

_____ A Los Angeles police report supports this advice.

_____ "Don't judge a book by its cover" means do not make a final judgement based on a first impression or just surface appearance.

_____ Dressed in a torn raincoat, stained sweatpants, and old running shoes with several toes poking out, she peered at the world through scraggly, dirty hair hanging over her weather-beaten face.

_____ In that city of movie stars a homeless woman, a bag lady, wandered the streets totally penniless.

_____ She always pushed a shopping cart full of bags, putting bits of food from a handout or a garbage can in them for a later meal.

_____ Public facilities served her bathroom needs.

_____ The beach was her bedroom in warm weather, doorways and the bus depot when the temperature dropped.

Body Paragraph

_____ But the real surprise came when the police searched her bags for identification.

_____ One afternoon she passed out on a crowded street.

_____ Taken to the poverty ward of the county hospital, she was diagnosed as suffering from untreated tuberculosis which had weakened her body to a life-threatening degree.

_____ A careful accounting later revealed that the women had given away the interest from all her investments, leaving nothing for herself.

_____ They also found cancelled checks showing huge contributions to charities such as the United Way and the American Cancer Society.

_____ They found stock and bond certificates totalling $750,000.

Body Paragraph

_____ She went wild buying clothing, jewelry, airline tickets, friends, cars, and other trinkets which brought her selfish pleasure.

_____ She explained that when she was twenty-three she had won two million dollars in a state lottery.

_____ When the press got wind of the news, reporters flocked to this unusual person's bedside to interview her for their readers and viewers.

(continued)

(continued)

_____ She was under seven minutes before a lifeguard pulled her to the surface and into a boat.

_____ One day, while swimming in the Pacific, she was gripped by a paralyzing cramp and sank beneath the water.

_____ Rushed to a hospital, she lay unconscious for five hours and was not expected to live.

_____ Then miraculously her eyes opened.

_____ A nurse spoke to her but she seemed not to hear.

_____ The next day she left the hospital and began her life of total self-sacrifice.

_____ She just stared into space and said, "Yes. Yes I will. I'll use it all to help."

Conclusion

_____ However, the Los Angeles bag lady impressed upon me most the need to suspend judgement about a person until you get to know him or her well.

_____ I have met people who looked honest but were really white collar criminals, who acted friendly but were really backstabbers, and who looked dull but turned out to be interesting, understanding friends.

_____ I have seen other examples where first impressions and appearances have been deceptive.

After students complete "Do Not Judge A Lady," they are given the following assignment for an original paper:

Pick another common saying. Several are listed below, but you can use a different one. Write about 250 words analyzing the saying by explaining what it means and giving one or more examples to show where it is or is not true.

The grass is always greener on the other side of the fence.
Different strokes for different folks.
Absence makes the heart grow fonder.
Bigger is better.
Look before you leap.
Haste makes waste.
Possession is nine-tenths of the law.
If you dance to the music, you must pay the piper.
You can't teach an old dog new tricks.
A bird in the hand is worth two in the bush.
Don't put all your eggs in one basket.
Pretty is as pretty does.

Asking students to give "one or more examples" frees them to deviate from the five-paragraph format and use any organization which lends coherence to their ideas and supporting details. They can use depth, breadth, or any mixture of specifics in supporting their meaning.

When students are assigned an original paper, they can begin by writing a few notes—not organized into a formal outline but just written as they come to mind—on ideas and details to include. Students who, after a few minutes of such brainstorming, feel they have enough material for a paper can start writing immediately. Others can brainstorm in pairs or groups for a few minutes to stir up opinions and experiences through discussion. This generally gives everyone enough material to start writing.

If students complete their papers at different times, the instructor may read them through quickly and discuss weak or strong points individually—perhaps suggesting additional development of an example; explaining a usage error and assigning a few pertinent exercises; or praising progress and commending effective writing. In combination with this, students can read other's papers in pairs or preassigned groups and offer suggestions for improvements before papers are rewritten to be handed in.

Students find it easier to think of something to write about after reconstructing several sample papers. Through organizing and copying, they see in fine detail how ideas are developed and supported. Sometimes sample papers can be used as springboards for original papers. The paper "Buffet Table" is a very basic, structured writing exercise.

SET 2 DESCRIPTION OF BUFFET TABLE

The following sentences can be arranged into an orderly description of this buffet table.

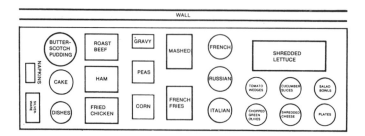

Exercise 1. Number the sentences so they systematically describe the buffet table, starting with the table's location and then moving from one end to the other.

_____ Next to these plates is the salad section.

_____ Moving past the salad dressings, you come to two pans of pota-toes: mashed in back and French fried in front.

_____ The buffet table is against the wall, so you can only serve your-self from the front.

_____ There is a large tub of shredded lettuce toward the back of the table, and in front there are four bowls with salad accom-paniments: tomato wedges, cucumber slices, chopped green olives, and shredded cheese.

_____ As you face the table, a stack of dinner plates and another stack of salad bowls are located at the right end.

_____ Finally, at the left end of the table there is a pile of napkins and a box with silverware.

_____ To the left of this are three metal containers with salad dress-ings: French closest to the wall, Russian in the middle, and Italian nearest the front.

_____ Next to the mashed potatoes is a pan of gravy, in front of this is a pan of peas, and closest to the front a pan of corn.

_____ This brings you to the desserts.

_____ To the left of these vegetables are three large meat trays, with roast beef in the back, fried chicken in front, and ham be-tween them.

_____ There is a large bowl of butterscotch pudding toward the back of the table, a platter of chocolate cake slices in the middle, and a stack of dessert dishes in front.

In one class, after students numbered the sentences and discussed their arrangements, they were told that, instead of just copying the sentences, they should include the buffet table in a larger paper. They were to imagine and describe a restaurant or other setting, eating alone or with anyone else, to narrate people's actions, and to add any items to the menu.

Some students brought their families to the buffet, one brought a date, and another made it the center of a wedding reception. Alcoholic drinks were available in one paper, so people got silly and sloppy serving food. Another paper included waiters who helped carry trays to tables, and the writer remembered to tip his waiter. Each student's background and personality had an opportunity to become expressed in the context of a structured human-interest story.

Much of what we write is not a model of pure description, narration, or general-specific organization. It is a mixture—a little description, a little narration, some comparison, all working to support our main point. This is explained to students, and they see many examples of such mixtures in longer TRC papers like "Step-parent Blues." If a student's interests or vocational aspirations involve writing, and he uses TRC exercises for several school semesters with writing samples from many sources, as memories for particular models blend and fade, what remains is the student's personal style.

TRC is not confined to recreating papers but can be used with various writing exercises. The following instructions and exercises from the workbook *Analytical Writing and Thinking* illustrate how TRC is used to help students think and write metaphorically.

Instructions

Effective writers use analogies as powerful tools for illustrating and explaining ideas. Standardized tests like the SAT use analogy questions for measuring reasoning ability.

In this chapter you will analyze analogies written by writers trying to paint vivid pictures for their readers. These are literary analogies, small pearls of creative and imaginative writing. When you identify the four terms in each analogy, you will have analyzed the analogy into the form used on standardized tests. Try filling the blanks for this analogy:

> Cynthia watched the new boy in class greedily, like a spider watching a fly it hoped to catch in its web.
>
> Cynthia: new boy as _____ : _____

The analogy says that Cynthia watched the new boy like a spider watches a fly. Here is how you could have filled the blanks.

> Cynthia: new boy as spider : a fly

The exercises which follow improve your ability to understand analogies, to use them in your writing, and to score well on standardized tests.

Exercises
Set 1   *Analyze Analogies*

In each exercise fill the blank(s) to show the terms in the analogy.

Your teacher may suggest that you work with a partner, taking turns reading the problems aloud and explaining the answers you write. Or you may be asked to work alone and then compare answers with a neighbor.

(continued)

(continued)

1. He was a popular mayor, but his thick eyebrows over his huge nose reminded me of heavy clouds encircling the peak of a mountain. Thick eyebrows : huge nose as _____ : _____

2. Like a charging elephant destroying trees in its path, the big fullback trampled opposing players on his way to the end zone.

   elephant: _____ as _____ : opposing players

3. She thought she could put her steady date aside in the summer and date other fellows, the way she put her textbooks on the shelf and read romantic novels.

   steady date: other fellows as _____ : _____

Etc.

Set 2 *Use Text Reconstruction for Writing Power*

How text reconstruction was used by professional writers to build their skills was described earlier. Use this powerful training method with the following analogies. After you analyze and analogy and fill in the blanks, follow these steps:

1. Read as much of the original analogy as you think you can write correctly from memory. Usually this will be between five and ten words.
2. Without looking at the book, write as much of the analogy as you can on a piece of paper.
3. Reread the analogy in the book. Then from memory, make corrections or additions to bring your version closer to the original.
4. Reread and revise from memory as often as necessary—sometimes four or five times—until your version is identical to the original.

1. Like a TV screen shattered by a hammer, her dreams collapsed when the riot destroyed her store.

   TV screen: hammer as _____ : _____

   Write the analogy from memory.
2. Dreams chased themselves around his mind all night like echoes bouncing around a cave.

   _____ : mind as echoes : _____

   Write the analogy from memory.

Etc.

Set 3. *Write Analogies*

Each exercise presents the terms from an analogy you analyzed. Write a literary analogy using the four terms wothout looking at the analogy you analyzed earlier. Yours does not have to use identical words or ideas.

(continued)

(continued)

1. charging elephant: trees as fullback : opposing players
2. TV screen: hammer as dreams : riot
3. dreams: mind as echoes : cave

Compare your analogies to their counterparts in the book by finding them in the previous sections. Do you like your wording or ideas better for some of them?

After going through this series of exercises, students tend to include more comparisons and metaphor in explaining their ideas and experiences.

TRC has been used with students ranging from elementary school to college level, and also with foreign adults learning English. Other TRC paragraphs teaching patterns of organization can be found in *Paragraph Play* by Levy and several workbooks including *English Skills with Readings* by Langan.

Teachers can create TRC exercises from any written material which is interesting or useful for students stretching from history or literature textbooks through current newspaper editorials on hotly debated subjects.

Students report they enjoy TRC because the assignments are clear and they see improvements in their writing. How many Franklins, Londons, and Maughams our educational system can produce when TRC is widely used may be a surprising bonus from a pedagogy playing the broader role of enabling schools to prepare a verbally and analytically strong work force capable of making the 21st century a golden age of technology.

CHAPTER 6

Writing, Talking, and Notetaking Across The Curriculum

> Although we ourselves have enthusiastically advocated writing across the curriculum and related reforms, we have found no convincing research base for these programs.

The above comment, made by Langer and Applebee in the Department of Education-sponsored report *How Writing Shapes Thinking*, reflects the current status of a nation-wide educational program known as *Writing Across the Curriculum* (WAC).

WAC refers to focusing on writing in courses besides English composition such as biology, history, literature, mathematics, and chemistry. WAC has several strong features, but in some ways it has been oversold. Also, it tends to shift the responsibility and accountability for teaching writing away from where they belong, the English class.

WAC—which has the goals of improving writing ability, reasoning skill, and course mastery in academic subjects—emerged from the same tradition and teachers that produced the process approach described in Chapter 4, partly to rectify the disappointing performance of the process approach in English classes.

As explained in Chapter 4, English teachers find the question "What should I write about?" a perennial problem with the process approach. So process theorists suggest that students use the approach for writing about the subject matter of other courses. Writing about the material in a history or chemistry class solves the problem of what to write about.

Also, process theorists are finding the process approach less effective than expected for strengthening students' writing and analytical skills in English classes. They maintain that the problem is that students are not writing enough in other classes. For example, regarding the poor writing performance of students on the National Assessment of Educational Progress, Langer and Applebee do not suggest that changes may be needed in English classes, such as using more sentence combining, but assert: "Put simply, in the whole range of academic course work, American children do not write frequently enough. . . ."

WAC LOST

A primary rationale for WAC is the claim that writing is a way of *discovering new knowledge, ideas, and insights.* The major evidence for the claim comes from reports by some professional writers that they are often surprised by what they write, that characters in their novels or plays develop independent personalities and control what the type-writer prints. Thurber paints such a picture in contrasting his work habits with those of a collaborator:

> Elliot Nugent . . . is a careful constructor. When we were working on *The Male Animal* together he was constantly concerned with plotting the play. He could plot the thing from back to front—what was going to happen here, what sort of situation would end the first-act curtain and so forth. I can't work that way. Nugent would say, "Well, Thurber, we've got our problem, we got all these people in the living room. Now what are we going to do with them?" I'd say that I didn't know and couldn't tell him until I sat down at my typewriter and found out. I don't believe the writer should know too much where he's going.

WAC proponents also cite the sayings of two Soviet psychologists, Vygotsky and Luria, to support their suppositions. Soviet psychology since Pavlov has been devoutly behavioristic—in accord with material-istic Communist philosophy—and interprets mental experiences as epiphenomena of physiological reactions and physical acts. Luria, for example, writes: "It is not understanding that generates the act (of writing), but far more the act that gives birth to understanding—indeed the act often far precedes understanding.".

Based on such comments, advocates of WAC believethat having students write about the subject matter of a course is the best way of helping them *create meaning,* adding to their depth of understanding while also improving analytical thinking ability. In "Definition of Writing to Learn" Toth elaborates:

Writing becomes a basic extension of the thinking process: discovering, imagining, evaluating, classifying, recalling, questioning, remembering, deciding, connecting, and hypothesizing.

As students learn how to use writing to learn, they discover that writing can work for them personally. Writing as thinking can serve them as a learning tool. The student's personal interactions with the reading content awakens memory, bonds a connection with prior knowledge, stimulates an awareness of what is known, and suggests what one may want to know about a subject.

WAC program director Soven confirms, "For more than ten years now we have urged our colleagues to view writing as both a thinking process and a powerful tool for stimulating creative thought." Such urgings caught the attention of educators in various academic disciplines seeking ways to improve students' content mastery as well reasoning and writing skills. WAC advocates wrote numerous articles and books and also conducted workshops suggesting ways for teachers to incorporate additional writing into their classes. Here are the most common suggestions:

1. Have students keep a learning log. Toth explains, "writing to learn proponents suggest a learning log as a place for students to write about their reading and their own experiences in reading. The learning log is a place for recording impressions. Here students may generate questions, think on many levels simultaneously, discover and record inner voice, metacognitively become aware of how they learn, and actually know how they know what they know."

2. Have students keep a class journal. At the end of a lecture over complicated material have the class spend five minutes writing about the main ideas of the lecture or listing any points of confusion. This will help students consolidate and clarify their knowledge. Also, if you collect the journals, you will have feedback on your lecture for planning the next one. (The terms *journal, log,* and *notebook* are used interchangeably in the WAC literature, with authors sometimes using one to refer to free writing about subjective feelings regarding class material and another for free writing about objective ideas and content. We also use the terms interchangeably.)

3. Precede lectures and discussions with a five-minute journal-write. Suggest a topic related to the day's lesson and let students write to bridge the gap between what they already know and the new material.

4. Assign term papers and focus on the writing process. Remember that students may pay little attention to comments written on a paper which has already been assigned a final grade. Have students write a first draft for the paper. Read through the drafts making comments about needed improvements in content or organization. Correct spelling and mechanical errors without making a fuss. Concentrate mainly on clarity and proper use of terms and concepts related to the course. Alternatively, reserve a class period to let students read each other's first drafts and make suggestions. Also, read and discuss a model paper so student know what is expected.
5. Assign short papers. For example, in a math class, let students write one-page research papers on mathematicians and their contributions. Again, focus on the writing process, commenting on organization and clarity of drafts.
6. Use letter writing. In an economics class, have students write letters to economic policy makers suggesting changes or reforms and methods for implementing the suggestions. In history, have students write letters to famous historical figures praising or castigating their actions and explaining any current ramifications. Of course, focus on the writing process, commenting hopefully, helpfully on drafts.
7. Have students keep a learning notebook. At appropriate times in class, stop other activities and let students write in their notebooks about their feelings. They should focus on their emotional reactions to the material being covered, guided by questions such as "How do I feel about the material?" "What did I already know about it?" "What confuses me? "How can I use the material?" and, according to Tschudi, "What makes me angry?" Provide tissues and tranquilizers should students become maudlin or agitated.
8. Have students keep an out-of-class response journal in which they spend five minutes outside of class writing about the main ideas of each lecture or listing any points of confusion.

How do students react to WAC? Couch shares a precaution with teachers to insure they *have* students to answer this question:

> A . . . concern is that if students are asked to write in courses they already consider difficult, they will be overwhelmed and may even drop the courses. There is some basis for this fear, but it need not be a major deterrent. Most instructors would agree that to impose heavy writing

assignments on students already challenged by terminology and concepts would be unwise.

Once students have been gingerly introduced to WAC, should teachers collect, correct, and grade their letters, logs, and papers? "Evaluating papers, like writing them, can be extremely time-consuming and wearing on one's nerves and spirit," intimates *Improving Student Writing: A Guidebook for Faculty in All Disciplines.* To reduce wear and tear on a teacher's nerves and time, Tschudi distinguishes between "personalized notes" and "journals."

> I teach my students what I call "personalized notetaking." Instead of copying down facts from texts or lectures, students should interact constantly with their material—critically, analytically, aesthetically, *personally.* Their notes should reflect their point of view as well as the content of a course. . . .

> A journal is more formal than a set of notes; it focuses on students' reactions to readings or lectures or discussion rather than emphasizing content.

Although the distinction between *notes* and *journals* may not be totally clear from these definitions, a teacher ought not be too rigid about this because, according to Tschudi, the former consumes less of his or her time:

> Personalized notes need not be read or evaluated by the instructor, although I usually collect the notebooks from time to time to see if students have the basic ideas. Personalized notes are generally a private piece of writer-based prose, however—an aid to the student in mastering the field (but providing a fringe benefit to everyone by increasing the amount of learn-by-doing writing being produced). . . .

> Although essentially writer-based, journals should also communicate with the instructor, who collects them from time to time for reading and response. I tell my students that I will not respond to every item in their journals (a task that would obviously be impossible with classes of any but seminar size). Rather, I scan the journals for highlights and to get a sense of the interaction with the course material that is taking place. I also invite students to star or asterisk items to which they particularly want a response from me.

In WAC students are told they should write without expecting class credit or teacher comments but solely for their improved understanding and course mastery; however, teachers find them generally unconvinced. Most students take an assignment seriously only if it is to be handed in and contributes in some way to their grade, claiming all courses place heavy demands on their time. Perhaps if WAC activities showed more dramatic benefits, students would find them more intrinsically motivating. As it stands, if teachers don't bother periodically collecting, evaluating, and crediting WAC assignments, students don't bother doing them. Describing one teacher's experience, Langer and Applebee say:

> At the beginning of the project, he tried to divorce the learning logs from the point system, emphasizing the value of the logs for their own sake. While fine in theory, in practice this approach made both teacher and students uncomfortable. The learning logs were not fully institutionalized until the following year, when they gained their own point value.

Another teacher graded all the writing he requested of students because "When you say it's a checkoff assignment, the kids say, 'Oh, okay,' and you get a laid-back attitude and you have to guard against that sort of thing."

The time and complexities involved in responding to students' papers is reflected by this discussion from the section "Strategies for Helping Students Write for Content Courses" in the text *Integrated Skills Reinforcement*.

> About errors, however, you have to be really careful, because pointing them out at very early draft stages is a mistake. When writers are still developing their ideas, they need to focus on logic and clarity of expression and not on spelling or on errors with subjects and verbs. Comments on first drafts generally should avoid discussion of language errors altogether. However, when students submit a draft beyond the first—and certainly when they submit their final manuscripts—you do need to call attention to mistakes.
>
> But you do not want to correct those mistakes. What is wrong with an instructor's correcting a student's error or with making other kinds of editorial changes on students' papers? In the first place, the students themselves should be the only ones to alter, finally, the language they have produced. . . .
>
> Thus the recommendation here is for you to call attention to problems and errors but not to make changes. Instead, identify problems in the margin next to the lines in which they appear, or raise questions about choices made by students in regard to language or syntax. For example:

You made two subject-verb agreement errors on this page.

Why did you use this word?

Why did you use a period here instead of a comma?

Some instructors circle or underline errors on the line so that students know which words need correction. To point out mistakes, others use conventional marking symbols with which students usually have had some experience in past English courses. (If you do use marking symbols, be sure to provide in your statement of your general writing requirements—see Strategy 15—a list of those symbols along with explanations of their meaning. . . .

In addition, the text suggests teachers write comments at the end of "early and intermediate drafts and on final manuscripts" explaining strengths and then weaknesses.

Integrated Skills Reinforcement was written by five teachers at LaGuardia Community College and presents the best available solutions to problems faced in implementing WAC. The critical comments in this chapter are directed at WAC, not at the work of sincere educators who have labored hard trying WAC as a last resort because better methods for teaching writing skills in English classes have not been available until recently.

Another view of the class time and student work involved in trying to seriously implement WAC is shown by this advice in *Integrated Skills Reinforcement* on how teachers can save their own time by having students provide feedback on writing.

Step 10: *Develop a collaborative situation in which students offer comments on each other's drafts.* A useful strategy is to arrange for peer feedback. Put students into groups: review the terms of the assignment; then ask each writer to read his or her draft aloud while the rest of the group takes notes on strengths and weaknesses in the expression of ideas. To guide constructive collaboration, you will find it helpful to prepare with the class a checklist of pointers to consider in reacting to drafts each time around. . . .

After each reader is finished, group members may discuss the draft with the author. Or you can arrange for groups of three to read papers and then to write commentary for their colleagues. With this plan each student takes home two critiques to guide revisions.

This description shows the time but not the problems involved in using students to provide feedback on papers. The problems encountered are so common and troublesome that Spear has written an entire book to deal with them entitled *Sharing Writing: Peer Response Groups in English Classes.* She divides problems with peer groups into five types: confusion over the purpose of the groups and the students' roles in them, inability to read group members' tests analytically, misperceptions about revision, inability to work collaboratively with groups, and failure to monitor and maintain group activity. Preparing students to reduce these problems takes time away from other class activities, which is a general objection that many teachers have to WAC. Glassman, summarizing an attempt to introduce WAC at Embry-Riddle Aeronautical University, reports, "In order to instill a writing-as-process attitude, the writing faculty member urged his partner to use collaborative techniques after the initial critiques came in. The management faculty member freely admitted her first attempt at inducing collaboration with her students was a flop. (She called it a 'bad experience.') But she saw the usefulness of the collaborative techniques and gamely vowed to try them in other semesters." If a *management* professor had trouble managing collaboration, one can understand difficulties encountered by other teachers.

Whimbey tried having students write in journals for 10 minutes at the end of each lecture in a psychology class in 1971 at Hayward State University. He had learned of the idea in a workshop at neighboring University of California, Berkeley.

Whimbey felt that the top 40% of his students generally learned class material adequately with the standard lecture-textbook format, but he was looking for a technique to improve the learning of weaker students. He collected and read sample journal entries but did not make comments because this would have taken time from other work and he understood it to be unnecessary, having read assurances like this from Fulwiler:

> A common objection . . . raised by classroom teachers is the amount of time it takes to assign and evaluate student writing, especially in large classes. However, recent composition theory supports, more strongly than ever, the importance of the writing students do strictly for themselves, writing the teacher need never see nor formally evaluate. I'm speaking, of course, about student journals, a time-honored form of writing which, when well used, is capable of revolutionizing classroom learning. . . . Assigning journals increases writing fluency, facilitates learning, and promotes cognitive growth, regardless of class size or disciplinary specialization.

In reading the journals, Whimbey found that the better students were generally able to write with understanding about basic concepts, whereas the poorer students had both weaker writing skills and less grasp of the material. However, the journals did not seem to appreciably improve skills or understanding over the course of the semester, so journal writing was not continued in future classes. Class time seemed better spent presenting concrete examples to illustrate difficult concepts or letting students work together solving problems based on taught principles. Although other teachers had similar experiences in the 1970s, WAC proponents have continued to publicize WAC—with creative abandon concerning lack of solid evidence—as the best thing since sliced bread, fooling one teacher or school after another into trying it. A typical example is a chemistry teacher who Langer and Applebee report in 1987 learned of WAC through the Bay Area Writing Project, whereupon she "tried using learning journals and had found them unsuccessful because the students did not focus on the critical issues, nor did they give her feedback to help her make constructive change in the curriculum."

In addition to journals and papers, WAC has another suggestion for math classes, explained by Couch: "Classes in mathematics frequently have few writing assignments. And yet at times students can be helped by writing out, step by step, the procedure they are following to solve a problem." Couch quotes Myers that "Gaps in learning can be spotted easily if students are asked to exchange papers and check each other's paper for accuracy."

To get a picture of the step-by-step procedure used in working a problem, an analytical student was asked to "think aloud" and explain his steps as he solved this one:

Fred is renovating a haunted house he bought. The kitchen is 20 feet long. For 14 of these 20 feet it is 9 feet wide, but because of the hidden passageway, it is only 7 feet wide for the remainder. How many square feet of Italian marble will Fred need to cover the floor?

Student Response
"I'm going to make a diagram of the room so I can see it. The problem says the room is 20 feet long, so I'll draw a room and write 20 along one wall."

20

"Next it says for 14 feet of the 20, the room is 9 feet wide. So I'll write 9 at this end."

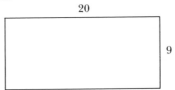

"And I'll come down 14 feet along this side—let's see. The whole length is 20. Half of 20 is 10. So 10 would be half the way down. Fourteen would be a little more than half. About three."

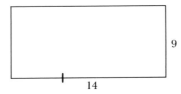

"It says the room is only 7 feet wide for the remainder, so I'll . . . 7 from 9 is 2 . . . so I'll go in 2 feet and then down to the end."

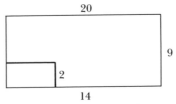

"The distance remaining to the end is 6 feet so I'll write that in."

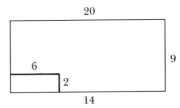

The problem solver continued to explain his steps in this way.

Students find that thinking aloud is initially a bit cumbersome, but they adjust to it quickly. However, they complain that writing all their observations, mental operations, and decisions is time consuming and tedious. They say it is "like writing a letter instead of marking a call. Calling is easier. You can work for half an hour writing a letter—or just make a relaxed ten-minute call." Furthermore, studies indicate that having students think aloud while solving problems can improve analytical ability and course mastery.

Bloom and Broder reported an experiment in which analytically weak students worked in pairs and took turns solving problems while thinking aloud. They were shown examples of how good reasoners work in small, careful steps to interpret material and answer questions, and they were told to work the same way. Thinking aloud reduced their tendency to skim material superficially and jump to conclusions. Instead they focused more on interpreting information carefully, synthesizing it to form an accurate overall picture, and reasoning in precise steps to reach a correct answer. Follow-up data showed that their new cognitive style resulted in improved grades on classroom tests.

This procedure, called thinking aloud pair problem solving, has been incorporated into the SOAR Project (described in Chapter 3)—the country's most successful program for helping minority students enter medical professions.[2] In addition, thinking aloud problem solving has been found useful in improving reading comprehension by Brown, mathematical ability by Lochhead, medical reasoning by Blanc, and problem-solving skills in chemical engineering by Woods.

Thinking aloud pair problem solving is just one form of a pedagogy called *collaborative learning* in which students work together to comprehend and apply academic material. In some classes, students work in groups of three (with a strong, average, and weak student in each group) as they master content and use it to answer questions. Numerous reports can be found in the professional literature on applications of collaborative learning in different schools.

Collaborative learning can be more effective than peer-response writing groups because its learning tasks can be better defined, and the skills required can be taught immediately before students attempt to apply them. With properly structured collaborative learning, students are only expected to help each other advance a small step beyond their current skills. In math, for instance, the teacher may spend 15 minutes introducing a topic and solving two sample problems. Then students can work increasingly more complex problems in a thinking aloud pair problem solving format, while the teacher circulates among them checking progress. This is more feasible for students than having them read each other's multiple-page papers and comment on everything from grammar and sentence structure to content and organization, requiring a large untaught knowledge base. Also, in collaborative

---

[2] Students or teachers interested in SOAR can write Professor Carmichael, Xavier University, New Orleans, LA 70125.

learning students do not feel they are criticizing each other as harshly as they do in making paper-revision suggestions with WAC.

Aside from the practical problems of WAC, its real unraveling is a fatal flaw of fiction for fact in its underlying theory. WAC is an educational edifice whose engineers claim it can support all academic disciplines, built on a cotton candy foundation.

WAC proponents profess the doctrine that people learn as they write—ideas are born as pens mate with pages. Writing is revered as a major route for discovering meaning, a way of knowing, a fountain of logic and inspiration. Invariably testimonials such as that by Thurber cited earlier are offered for support. Thurber is the creator of Walter Mitty, a gentle little man who daydreamed fantastic, exciting worlds in which he was a stunning hero and systems like WAC could work. The point is that the testimonials presented as factual evidence are invariably fiction writers' reports. Writing as described by Thurber is not a way of creating knowledge but fiction; it is not learning but fantasizing. Scientists seldom describe themselves sitting down at the word processor devoid of ideas and then watching a research report come out at their fingertips. In *The Double Helix*, Watson describes the activities that led to his discovery of the structure of DNA—observing, model-building, discussing, calculating, and drawing:

> Three days later the phosphorous atoms were ready, and I quickly strung together several short sections of the sugar-phosphate backbone. Then for a day and a half I tried to find a suitable two-chain model with the backbone in the center. All the possible models compatible with the B-form X-ray data, however, looked stereochemically even more unsatisfactory than our three-chained models of fifteen months before.
> . . .
>
> There was no difficulty in twisting an externally situated backbone into a shape compatible with the X-ray evidence. In fact, both Francis and I had the impression that the most satisfactory angle of rotation between two adjacent bases was between 30 and 40 degrees. . . . Francis' interest began to perk up, and at increasing frequencies he would look up from his calculations to glance at the model. . . .
>
> My doodling of the bases on paper at first got nowhere . . .
>
> Not until the middle of the next week, however, did a nontrivial idea emerge. It came while I was drawing the fused rings of adenine on paper. Suddenly I realized the potentially profound implications of a DNA structure in which the adenine residue formed hydrogen bonds similar to those found in crystals of pure adenine. If DNA was like this, each adenine residue would form two hydrogen bonds to an adenine residue related to it by a 180-degree rotation. Most important, two symmetrical hydrogen bonds could also hold together pairs of guanine,

cytosine, or thymine. I thus started wondering whether each DNA molecule consisted of two chains with identical base sequences held together by hydrogen bonds between pairs of identical bases.

When a scientist writes up his findings, he continues to think and sometimes has new insights. But such insights-while-writing are just one source of a nonfiction writer's ideas. Archimedes was not sitting at his desk writing but up to his waist in tub water when he formulated the principle of liquid displacement and went running through the streets of Syracuse clothed only in a bath towel yelling "Heureka! Heureka!" Surrounded by water, he discovered something about water. Similarly Edison, surrounded by electricity, made discoveries about electricity. So writers writing, surrounding themselves with forms of expressing ideas, may discover a new way to express some idea—a way that makes an argument more convincing or an explanation more understandable. They discover something about writing, not about the physics of fluids or electricity. The greatest proportion of learning-while-writing concerns forms of expression and fictional plots, not the topics to which WAC generally addresses itself such as principles of chemistry. Langer and Applebee in *How Writing Shapes Thinking* note that, if the assumptions of WAC are correct, "if writing is so closely related to thinking, we might expect to be able to cite a variety of studies that support the contribution of writing to learning and instruction. Yet recent reviews of the relevant literature . . . make it obvious that there has been little research on this issue". WAC is based on the assumption "that the process of writing will in some inevitable way lead to a better understanding of the topic under consideration, though how this comes about tends to be treated superficially and anecdotally". Langer and Applebee conclude that more "research is essential before we can knowledgeably suggest that asking students to write is an important part of the teaching of subject-area content, not just a favor to the English department".

The strong emphasis on writing about reactions and feelings to create personal meaning—the legacy of focusing on fiction for facts about writing—has led WAC to overlook or slight one of the most effective forms of writing to improve learning.

WAC REGAINED

Taking notes while reading textbooks is among the oldest yet best ways of using writing to improve learning. It is also, ironically, the one writing activity WAC has neglected to encourage because of its stress on having students write freely, express impressions, and use the process approach to create their own meaning.

In a major review of the research literature, Stotsky found that "A number of studies, old and new, suggest the usefulness of . . . [taking notes, outlining, and summarizing] for improving comprehension or retention of information in reading material." She adds "those who seek to improve reading through writing activities or writing instruction may be most successful with writing exercises that entail the reading of instructional texts. Writing instruction and writing activities designed primarily to improve free writing may have some effect on reading comprehension but, apparently, not a great one . . ."

In other words, research indicates that simply taking notes on a text—writing key terms and paraphrasing main ideas while reading— seems to be at least as effective for improving comprehension and recall as the activities recommended by WAC. These are exemplified by Sears' suggestion that students free-write after reading assignments, focusing on these points: What questions came to mind as you read? What memories or associations occurred? What seems most or least important and why? How did you respond to difficult passages?

Since notetaking on textbooks improves content mastery, teachers might make this a required part of courses—particularly social studies and literature courses which, in contrast to math and science courses, involve extensive reading without opportunities for application in problem solving. The question is, how can students be encouraged to take notes on textbooks regularly? The answer, like a phoenix rising out of the ashes, is the most valuable insight to emerge from WAC.

Students neglect it unless teachers collect it—this is the lesson learned from WAC with a direct application to notetaking. Students tend to neglect writing assignments unless teachers collect, evaluate, and credit them toward course grades. Most students do not make the effort to write just for its own benefits, even when the benefits are as evident as from taking textbook notes. Students need a little extra prodding, an immediate, concrete reward.

Based on what Langer and Applebee report that WAC teachers found they need to do to elicit writing, a teacher could collect the notes (the more frequently the better, preferably every class), write comments about anything missing, misunderstood, or well expressed, and enter credit in the grade book—either just a check or a 1-2-3 rating. The accumulated credits might raise a student's grade as much as one letter grade.

Students need not be taught any formal notetaking system with capital and small letters, arabic and Roman numerals, or other labels for headings. However, it might be helpful for the teacher to display a set of good notes from a student text assignment on an overhead projector and read through them, so students have an understanding and model of notetaking. This can be done early in the course and, if needed, again as part of preparing for tests, because it reviews course content. While paraphrasing the text is generally preferable, when a student is not able to paraphrase because of comprehension or language difficulties, copying a sentence or two verbatim might be the most beneficial alternative. To give students additional help, Heiman and Slomianko have developed a program that teaches them how to take notes which focus on the integrated meaning of lectures and textbooks by asking crucial questions of the material.

At the elementary school level, a form of WAC that is proving useful is to have youngsters copy material in various content areas— have them copy math word problems, textbook summaries, homework assignments, and even questions on tests. This is supported by the research reviewed in Chapter 5 on the benefits of copying for writing skills.

According to Jordan and Moorhead, a survey of non-English faculty at Eastfield College in Dallas revealed that "50+ percent were interested in having students write in their classes, that 74 percent agreed with the philosophy of WAC, but that only 5 percent would assign more writing if they were provided some assistance by the English faculty."

While non-English faculty do not want to assign *more* writing, they are generally quite receptive to any help English teachers can offer with the writing that is already a part of their courses. WAC is now taking on a broader, less prescriptive role. Teachers from English departments help in various ways to communicate the importance of strong writing skills to students and faculty in all areas, and a number of new activities are being subsumed under the WAC umbrella. Jordon and Moorhead report, for example, that an English professor paired through a WAC program with an economics professor helped develop "a seminar presentation for economics students (and others) on summary and letter writing" and "a grading grid for drafts of papers and letters and for final products to ease grading chores." Another English teacher, paired with a child development instructor/program coordinator "worked with her as she rewrote course competency expectations for the two dozen courses offered in the child development program. In addition, he assisted her in the formulation of research topics, in their wording, and in the analysis/evaluation of the finished products."

Glassman of Embry-Riddle Aeronautical University reflects:

For a variety of reasons, we found while implementing a partner approach to writing across curriculum that, as in nouveau cuisine and waistlines, less is more. An intense application of WAC sometimes had the adverse effect of developing student antipathy, overburdening both partners and, to a noticeable extent, creating disharmony among a curriculum partner's department mates.

Glassman entitled his paper "The Light Touch: Minimal Applications of the Partner Approach to Writing Across the Curriculum", and recommended that WAC instructors help other teachers develop better methods for making and evaluating writing assignments. This may include helping them formulate and clarify assignments, providing handouts on the format of required papers and other writing topics, speaking to students about writing topics (especially the importance of revision), and imparting a better understanding of grading papers. He concludes:

> The results of our experience indicate that anyone interested in putting a partner-oriented WAC program in place would probably be best served by leaving the heavy-duty writing instruction in the English classroom and concentrating on minimal contact and assignments with across-curriculum partners.

Looking at this another way, two methods for improving writing, WAC and sentence combining, have now accumulated two decades of research suggesting that increasing the use of SC in English classes is a more effective way to improve students' writing skills than wasting the time of English teachers on large-scale WAC projects.

CHAPTER 7

Thoughts and Chickens

A number of issues in the teaching of writing touch on the relationship between thinking and language: Are words just vehicles of thought? Is writing a form of thinking? Is forming verbalizations the essense of thinking? Pages upon pages of theories are concocted and quoted in scholarly texts. Names of purported Russian experts such as Vygotsky and Luria are splashed around like imported, heady, high-proof vodka. But in truth, available research offers not even a hint for answering these theoretical questions.

We do know that speed-reading programs give students bad advice in insisting that lip movement and subvocal speech should be suppressed while reading. Vocalizing can improve comprehension, contribute to appreciation of literary devices like alliteration, and help develop a student's ear for the language. Derelicts walking around city streets talking loudly into the air are as different from students moving their lips while reading science, drafting sentences, or solving math problems as lightning is from TV signals. Lip movements or other vocal activities while reading and thinking are often beneficial, not signs of mental derangement or deficiency. Furthermore, thinking-aloud problem solving seems to be useful for improving reasoning skills.

We know that words from the outside—from other people—give rise to and precede some of our thoughts, and it seems that often words from the inside do this as well. On the other hand, we have mental pictures, feelings, and tip-of-the-tongue experiences suggesting that at times thoughts precede words.

Viewing the puzzle as a chicken-and-egg phenomena has functional ramifications: Rather than worry, relentlessly hypothesize, and neurologically jargonize about the exact language-thinking connection, we should perfect and employ pedagogies which prove empirically effective for encouraging expertise in each, and depend on intrinsic relations for natural interactions. For example, instead of using WAC and the process approach because of their supposedly sophisticated underlying linguistic-theoretical pillars on mind, use sentence combining because it improves writing skills—expressed in loose anapest:

Mutter and Farther Go Thoughts

Do words produce thoughts,
Or do thoughts produce words?
Is the mind made of pictures,
Or nouns, preps, and verbs?
"The chicken came first!"
"No, the egg!" claims another.
It's confused beyond words,
Theorists stutter and mutter.

Take care of your chickens.
Your eggs will be better.
Keep your eggs warm and safe.
Your chickens will fine feather.

Take care of them both,
And for growth here's an oath:
When you speak to explain
Don't refrain if you stutter.
And while reading or thinking
Freely whisper and mutter.

Our mind is a mystery
Our mind knows little about.
But with words, thoughts expand:
Talk freely—inside and out.

CHAPTER 8

Inquiry Approach

A relatively new method for teaching writing, called *inquiry,* received an A+ grade in the NCTE survey of writing research. In fact, the editor of the report, Hillocks of the University of Chicago, conducted several studies on inquiry with impressive results.

The inquiry method begins by having students thoroughly examine and discuss some specific material or topic. For example, students may discuss the differences in appearance of several sea shells. Then the students write about the subject. Finally, they receive comments and constructive criticism on what they have written. Here is the summary of one study:

> Hillocks asked ninth- and eleventh-graders to observe a variety of phenomena carefully and to write about them as specifically as possible. The phenomena included seashells, objects with various textures, odors, sounds, bodily sensations, the actions of people, and so forth. Lessons usually involved teacher-led or small-group discussion prior to writing. Thus, in an exercise calling on students to describe sounds, teachers played a tape-recorded sound and called for students to suggest several words and phrases to describe it. This procedure was repeated with several sounds before students were asked to write about sound on their own. Eventually students wrote about some experience or place in a composition which incorporated sounds and other sensations. Teachers were asked to praise effective detail, clear focus, and overall impact. These implicit criteria were emphasized in class and in comments and suggestions on writing.
>
> In addition, students regularly shared their writing with small groups

or in pairs, often in view of some rhetorical context. For example, small groups wrote a composition about one or two seashells, then passed the writing and the shells to a second group. The second group identified the shell described by the first group and picked out vivid details in the writing as well as details they found confusing. In another exercise each student wrote a description of a shell. The teacher then placed all the shells on a table and delivered each composition to another student, who had to pick out the shell described. The reader then commented on effective detail and metaphor before returning the paper to the writer.

Compositions by students in the experimental groups were judged significantly superior to those by control-group students, who studied model paragraphs. A second panel of five judges, using their own criteria, rated a subset of pretests and postests from the same students for creativity. Their combined scores correlated highly with the earlier scale scores . . ., suggesting that creativity can be stimulated (if not taught) by such classroom experiences.

Hillocks points out several differences between the inquiry method and free writing of the type often used with the process approach described in Chapter 4.

While free writing avoids any specific topic suggestions, inquiry does not. While free writing requires students to recall more or less distant experience, inquiry tends to focus on immediate and concrete data of some kind during instruction and practice. While free writing implicitly requires students to use whatever strategies they have available, inquiry attempts to teach specific strategies.

The "specific strategies" are described by Hillocks as "strategies for dealing with data in order to say or write something about it." These develop through manipulating and discussing the material: Inquiry "activities are designed to enhance particular skills or strategies such as formalizing and testing explanatory generalizations, observing and reporting significant details to achieve an effect, or generating criteria for contrasting similar phenomena."

Finally, because students write about a specific, common topic, peer feedback can be more effective with inquiry than with the process approach. Note in the above example how students decide which of two shells other students depicted in writing, giving them a concrete basis for pointing out strengths and weaknesses. By contrast, with the process approach students have no objective criteria for evaluating papers, so their comments are subjective, vague, and sparse.

Another successful study of the inquiry approach was conducted by Troyka. Students prepared to write on topics by playing simulation games requiring them to make policy decisions about problems such as how to handle a community pollution problem, what action to take in a prison riot, and what automobile to purchase for a taxi fleet. Hillocks explains:

> Each student received a role sheet along with whatever background information he or she might need. The games were set up so that students were associated with a subgroup: executives of a chemical plant responsible for polluting a town's beaches and recreational waters, operators of tourist services who believed that pollution harmed the town's prosperity, and so forth. Each role had built into it the task of persuading the other groups of the legitimacy of its position on the problem. As the game progressed, the action alternated between periods of group planning and periods of "cross subgroup public hearings, debates, and the like. . . ." Presumably, these "games" put students in the position of using strategies required by the associated writing assignments: marshalling and arranging facts, evaluating and using reasons, examining and generating examples, predicting objections and considering how to deal with them, and so forth.

These students improved significantly more in writing skill than a group that was taught to use facts, reasons, and comparisons conventionally but did not actively discuss and debate issues.

The inquiry method comes closer to duplicating the process effective writers use for most real-life writing than the activities described in Chapter 4 which parade as the "process approach." In inquiry students spend considerable time researching and discussing a subject before beginning to write. They gather content, patterns of explanation and organization, and topic-specific language to eventually cast into standard written English. The act of writing forces them to extend their thinking in organizing and verbalizing the information, and gives them an opportunity to experiment and become familiar with various syntactic forms.

The only bridle on thundering enthusiasm for inquiry is the need to see how it fares in large-scale usage—whether any classroom management problems or other difficulties arise as the procedure is tried more widely with various class sizes, age levels, and ability groups. If big classes present management problems with elaborate inquiry tasks, simpler tasks might be tried which retain some of the essential characteristics of inquiry described by Hillocks:

> Inquiry focuses the attention of students on strategies for dealing with sets of data, strategies which will be used in writing. For example, . . .

inquiry might involve students in the following: . . . examining sets of data to develop and support explanatory generalizations, or analyzing situations which present problems of various kinds and developing arguments about those situations.

Our workbook, *Analytical Writing and Thinking,* uses analogy exercises which are easy for a teacher to handle yet have inquiry characteristics. Students are asked to work in pairs thinking aloud as they solve analogy questions (ostensibly as practice to raise their Scholastic Aptitude Test scores):

police : crime as _____ : _____
a. lawyers : law books   c. dentists : tooth decay
b. doctors : heart patient   d. lawyers : client

Students are first shown sample think-aloud responses from good problem solvers.

Thinking Aloud Problem Solving

"Police-crime. Police deal with crime."

"Lawyers-law books. Lawyers use law books, but police don't use crime."
"Doctors-heart patient. Doctors deal with a heart patient, and police deal with crime. They both work on a problem, so this could be an analogy."

"Dentists-tooth decay. Dentists try to stop—they fight tooth decay, and police fight crime. Tooth decay and crime are bad. This answer is better than doctors-heart patient. A heart patient isn't bad. His heart disease is bad. Doctors don't fight a heart patient."

"The last choice is lawyers-client. Lawyers don't try to stop or eliminate a client."

"Answer c forms the best analogy."

Students are also asked to write sentences showing how the pair of words they select for an answer parallels the initial pair in the analogy. Again they are shown a sample think-aloud response:

Writing Relationship Sentences

"I need to write a sentence relating police and crime. Police deal with crime. I'll write that."

He wrote: Police deal with crime.

"Now I have to write a sentence about dentists and decay. I could write dentists deal with decay. Wait a minute. I have to write more than 'deal with.' Otherwise answer b (answer-heart patient) will seem OK too."

"I have to write police fight crime. Then I can write dentists fight tooth decay."

He wrote: Police fight crime.
Dentists fight tooth decay.

Students are told that writing relationship sentences is not always easy, that even professional writers report they often encounter difficulty when they first try to express an idea in writing and may have to think for a while before satisfactory wording comes to mind; and that even after they have written a sentence, they often reread it and see a smoother or more effective way to communicate their meaning, so they cross out part or all of their first sentence and write a revised version. Students are shown samples of revision, such as this think-aloud response from a problem solver who chose answer c for the analogy:

stork : babies as _____ : _____

a. mailman : letters
b. messenger : telegrams

c. Santa : gifts
d. delivery man : groceries

Writing Process

"I have to write about relationship sentences. Let's see—a stork is said to bring babies. But that is just a myth. Santa is a mythical person that brings toys. And the stork is a mythical creature that brings babies. I can write that."

He wrote: 1. A stork is a mythical creature that brings babies.
2. Santa is a mythical creature that brings gifts.

"Wait. A stork isn't a mythical creature. Santa is mythical, but a stork is real. It is a myth that the stork brings babies. And it is a myth that Santa brings toys. I'll write that."

He wrote: 1. According to myth, storks bring babies.
2. According to myth, Santa brings toys.

Through the strong, albeit temporary, motivation to score well on the SAT, students mold skills to use for analyzing and expressing relationships in writing, skills which are building blocks for broad literacy. Other analytical writing tasks also have inquiry characteristics. Text reconstruction, for example, smacks of inquiry because students examine information and discuss arranging it into written form.

Inquiry imparts a skill for conceptualizing ideas and also the language for expressing them. The other technique rated most highly by the NCTE survey of writing instruction, sentence combining, develops craftsmanship—skill to shape sentences in various ways and combinations. The two methods together—with materials at the appropriate language level—would form a solid foundation for any composition class.

CHAPTER 9

Teaching Usage
and Functional Grammar

Writing Instruction in the Two-Year College, an Educational Resources Information Center (ERIC) digest which "draws upon the thirteen published volumes of *Inside English* to offer a summary of practitioners' advice on techniques to improve two-year college students' writing skills," concludes that "isolated drills in usage, formal grammar, phonics, and spelling have little value . . .," but "drills may be useful following diagnosis of weakness in a specific area. . . .". Furthermore, "sentence building is more productive than analysis or labelling."[3]

Chapter 2 illustrates why formal grammar instruction is ineffective. By contrast, the following exercises from *Analytical Writing and Thinking* show how an intuitive feeling for what constitutes a complete sentence is conveyed through the whole-language experience of letting students first correct comma splice errors (in which the comma divides the sentences) and then run-on errors, in which they must choose the division point.

Comma Splice Errors

On the highway a red light means stop. A blinking yellow light means slow down. In writing, a period means stop while a comma means slow down.

People are accustomed to finding a period at the end of a sentence.

---

[3] *Inside English* is published by the English Council of the California Two-Year Colleges.

When they come to a comma, they expect the next group of words to continue the same sentence rather than start a new sentence. If a comma is followed by a whole new sentence, readers become momentarily confused and have to stop, get reoriented, and then mentally start again.

The example below is not a correct sentence. It is two sentences with only a comma between them.

The luckiest couple was Adam and Eve, they had no in-laws.

This is called a comma splice error because two sentences are spliced (joined) by a comma.

Part 1 *Correct with a Period and Capital Letter*

There are several ways to correct a comma splice. Often the easiest is just to separate the sentences by putting a period at the end of the first one and a capital letter at the beginning of the second. Here is the correction of the above comma splice:

The luckiest couple was Adam and Eve. They had no in-laws.

Exercises

Correct each comma splice by putting a period at the end of the first sentence and a capital letter at the beginning of the second. Write the two corrected sentences.

1. I always wear sunglasses when it rains, they protect my eyes from the umbrellas.
2. Bigamy means having two wives, having more than two wives is pigamy.
3. Drugs are not a gamble, in gambling you win sometimes.
4. I stepped away from a laundry machine in Las Vegas for just three minutes, somebody won my wash.

Part 2 *Correct with a Semicolon*

If two sentences contain closely related ideas, you can separate them with a semicolon. Think of a semicolon as a weak period. It shows that two sentences are closely related. Here is how a comma splice is corrected with a semicolon.

Wrong: Never buy anything with a handle, it means work.
Right: Never buy anything with a handle; it means work.

Notice that when you use a semicolon, you do not capitalize the first letter in the second sentence.

Exercises

For each exercise, write the two sentences separated by a semicolon.

1. He does not make a fool of himself all the time, he has to rest occasionally.
2. My child has sensitive ears, he screams when I pull them.
3. Thirty-five was a difficult age to pass, it took four years.

Run-on Sentences

When you speak to someone, you pause at the end of each sentence. The pause shows that you are ending one idea and starting another one. When you write, you usually put a period at the end of each sentence. Otherwise you may produce a run-on sentence such as this one:

> Misfortune is a point of view your headache feels good to an aspirin salesman.

This run-on sentence is confusing because it presents two ideas that run together.

Run-on sentences can be corrected in the same ways you corrected comma splices: by adding a period and a capital letter, or by adding a semicolon. Here is how the above run-on could be corrected.

> Misfortune is a point of view. Your headache feels good to an aspirin salesman.

Part 1 *Correct with a Period and Capital Letter*
   The example above shows how to correct a run-on error by separating the sentences with a period and capital letter. Use this method for the following exercises.

Exercises
Rewrite each of the following run-on sentences correctly with a period and capital letter.

1. There is a new perfume that is guaranteed to drive businessmen crazy it smells like money.

2. It is not easy to get a parking ticket in New York first you have to find a place to park.

3. My parents did not want me they gave me a live teddy bear to play with in my crib.

4. In a group of barbers, always pick the one with the worst haircut they cut each other's hair.

The above lesson shows how usage problems can sometimes be corrected without the introduction of any grammatical terminology. In the next lesson, it is convenient to introduce the terms *verb* and *tense*. But students are not asked to label verbs in sentences. The grammar is learned informally and incidentally to mastering correct-usage patterns.

VERB PROBLEMS: TENSE AND FORM

Verbs are complicated to study, not because some ancient, devious grammar teacher conjured conjugations to confuse English students, but because as English developed over the centuries, it adopted words and language patterns from several early languages in an unplanned, unruly way. If you do not like the messy maze of English grammar, write your congressman to legislate language simplification the way Congress tried to mandate metric utilization. For now, this chapter will review some principles of verbs which are unavoidably complicated but will help you avoid errors in your own writing and on tests.

Part 1 *Regular Verbs*
   What is the difference between the underlined words in these two sentences?

> I <u>walk</u> to school today.
> I <u>walked</u> to school yesterday.

The -*ed* added to *walk* in the second sentence shows that the action of walking took place in the past.
   Words representing actions, such as *walk,* are called *verbs.* Verbs change their spelling to show when an action takes place—the time of the action. In grammar the time shown by a verb is called the *tense* of a verb.
   Most verbs (called regular verbs) have -*d* or -*ed* added to show that action occurred in the past. For words that end in *e,* just -*d* is added. Otherwise -*ed* is added (final consonants are sometimes doubled if preceded by vowels). Here are examples:

Present		*Past*
dance	Add -*d*	danced
stack	Add -*ed*	stacked
step	Add -*ed* (double p)	stepped

In the following table, notice that -*s* is sometimes added to *walk* in the present tense, as explained in a previous chapter. But -*s* is never added in the past tense.

Present Tense
I walk.   You walk.   We walk.
Carla walks.   She walks.   He walks.   A cow walks.
Carl and Katie walk.   They walk.

Past Tense
I walked.   You walked.   We walked.
Carla walked.   She walked.   He walked.   A cow walked.
Carl and Katie walked.   They walked.

Use these patterns in doing the following exercises.

Exercises
Each exercise has three sentences with one blank in each sentence. Fill each blank with the correct form of the verb given in parenthesis at the beginning of the exercise. The first exercise has been done as an example.

1. (COMB) I _comb_ my hair before leaving for work. My son Sammy _combs_ his hair before leaving for school. Last night we both _combed_ our hair before going to bed.

2. (DECIDE) Every morning I _____ which soap operas to record to watch in the evening. Sometimes my husband _____ on sports programs to record also. Last week, though, we _____ to record the PBS special on silent movies.

3. (TYPE) I _____ a diary entry every day into my computer. My sister usually _____ a daily entry into her computer too. My other sister _____ entries until she went to France last year.

4. (SHOP) I _____ once a week in the nearby supermarket. My roommate _____ through the week for whatever else we need. Last week we both _____ a total of six times.

Research suggests it is generally best to assign usage correction exercises on the basis of diagnosed need. Rather then make a blanket assignment for an entire class to do exercises on verb tense or pronoun problems a teacher may reserve such exercises only for students whose papers show they have difficulty in these areas.

The above exercises are from *Analytical Writing & Thinking: Facing the Tests,* which is designed to improve general writing and reasoning skills. However, the book has the ostensible goal of raising students' Scholastic Aptitude Test and high school graduation writing-test scores, and some students voluntarily cover all the chapters in the book rather than pay several hundred dollars to a test-preparation company like Kaplan's. In completing all of the chapters on usage problems, students often learn worthwhile knowledge or techniques for expressing themselves effectively in writing.

But such a blanket program should not be forced on students who do not have the intrinsic motivation of wanting to score well on some test. Normally students may just be assigned to usage chapters covering areas in which they make errors in the papers they write.

While drills may be useful following the diagnosis of specific weaknesses, drills are not a substitute for whole-language experiences such as sentence combining and text reconstruction, in which students read and write complete communication units—sentences and paragraphs—in standard written English. In explaining SC patterns, it is sometimes convenient to introduce grammatical terminology. Here again, the grammar is presented in a functional rather than formal way, as shown in this example from *Analyze, Organize, Write:*

Combining Sentences Having The Same Subject Or Predicate

A complete sentence always has two parts: (a) A subject; and (b) Information about the subject (called the *predicate*). Here is an example.

Willy went to the store.

Subject   Predicate (information about the subject).

When two sentences have the same subject, they often can be combined into one sentence with the word "and" like this.

The ship hit a rock.
The ship started to sink.

Combined: The ship hit a rock and started to sink.

Three sentences with the same subject can be combined with commas and the word "and" like this.

The cookies in the jar are freshly baked.
The cookies in the jar are filled with chocolate chips.
The cookies in the jar are so soft they melt in your mouth.

Combined: The cookies in the jar are freshly baked, filled with chocolate chips, and so soft they melt in your mouth.

If two sentences have different subjects but the same predicate, they also may be combined with "and," as shown here.

Roses are used in making perfumes.
Violets are used in making perfumes.

Combined: Roses and violets are used in making perfumes.

Three sentences with different subjects but the same predicate can be combined by using commas along with "and."

Democrats want lower taxes.
Republicans want lower taxes.
Independents want lower taxes.

Combined: Democrats, Republicans, and Independents want lower taxes.

The following exercises illustrate additional opportunities for combining sentences with the same subject or predicate.

EXERCISES

Instructions. Combine the sentences in each exercise by using "and" along with any necessary commas. Use the examples just given as models.

1. Monsters live in the cellar.
   Monsters eat children.

   Combined:

2. A hot bath will make you feel better.
   A warm meal will make you feel better.
   A good rest will make you feel better.

   Combined:

3. The quarterback studied the plays.
   He practiced them for hours.
   He executed them perfectly at the game.

   Combined:

Note that the exercises are not drills on grammatical nomenclature. They avoid terminology and focus completely on using language.

While SC does not try to teach grammar, it may impart a strong understanding of grammatical concepts. Prepositions, for example, are not easy to pin down with an explicit definition. In a typical grammar lesson, prepositions are defined as words showing relationships, particularly with respect to space and time, and then a representative list is presented—usually including *before, after, above, below, for* and *of*—for students to memorize.

The words *for* and *of* are different from *above* and *after*. For one thing, they are not about space and time. In trying to understand exactly what prepositions are, you might look back to the definition which says they are "words showing *relationships.* . . ." But consider this sentence: Bob has *more* marbles than Ted. The word *more* represents a relationship between quantities, yet in this sentence it is not a preposition but an adjective.

SC gives students a sense of what prepositions are by experiencing how they function in a sentence, as illustrated in this lesson.

Prepositions (handwritten margin note)

Combining Sentences With Prepositional Phrases

Prepositions are words like "in," "under," "after," "to," "of," and "without" that are used to describe relationships between things, such as spatial and time relationships. Here is a sentence with three prepositions underlined.

Bob went <u>to</u> the store <u>in</u> the truck <u>after</u> dinner.

A prepositional phrase is a phrase starting with a preposition. In the above sentence, the three prepositional phrases are:

to the store
in the truck
after dinner

Combining prepositional phrases is one way to lengthen sentences. The prepositional phrases are underlined in the following examples.

Example 1.

The new girl sat <u>by Bob</u>.
They sat <u>on the sofa</u>.
The sofa was <u>near the window</u>.

Combined: The new girl sat by Bob on the sofa near the window.

Example 2.

The young boy was racing.
He was racing <u>across the glistening ice</u>.
He was <u>from the hockey club</u>.
He was racing <u>with new skates</u>.

Combined: The young boy from the hockey club was racing across the glistening ice with new skates.

Note that "from the hockey club" is placed after "boy" and "across the glistening ice" is placed after "racing." Place prepositional phrases where the information they add will be understood most clearly.

Now try these exercises.

EXERCISES

Instructions. For each exercise, lengthen the first sentence by adding the prepositional phrases from the other sentences. Here are the prepositions to look for.

in, with, from, under, after, for, to, on, during, of, next, across

1. The boat sank.
   The boat was in the harbor.
   It sank with the diamonds still aboard.

   Combined:

2. Juanita got the pistol and bullets.
   She got them from the shoe box.
   The shoe box is under the bed.
   She did this after Willy left.
   He left for work.

   Combined:

3. The teacher sent Bob upstairs when she caught him writing.
   She sent him to the principal's office.
   She sent him with a note.
   The note was in a sealed envelope.
   He was writing on the wall.
   He was writing in black crayon.
   It was during recess.

   Combined:

Seeing where prepositions can be inserted in sentences—and the information they introduce—builds an operational understanding of the linguistic similarity shared by prepositions and an intuitive sense of what they are as a class.

Drawing together his own research and that of Mellon, Cooper concludes that usage correction coupled with sentence combining is more effective for improving writing skill than formal grammar instruction:

> My considered opinion is that teachers should be using . . . sentence-combining problems on a regular basis with their students. Used with an informal approach in correcting deviancy from standard English usage and punctuation, they permit the teacher to guiltlessly eliminate the teaching of a formal grammar, since both these activities—informal approach to deviancy and sentence-combining problems—fulfill the traditional goals of a grammar study: standard usage and control of written syntax.

CHAPTER 10

Additional Sentence Combining Ideas

As virtual civil war raged between Azerbaijanis and Armenians, the Kremlin on Monday declared a state of emergency and sent units of the Soviet army, navy and KGB security service to the troubled southern region, where the Kremlin said attempts were being made "to overthrow Soviet power."

—Steve Goldstein,
Knight-Ridder News Service

A sentence such as that above is never found in the essays of weak writers. Here is an example of the type of paper given a *minimal* rating on the National Assessment of Educational Progress:

I have been experience at cleaning house. I've also work at a pool be for. I love keeping things neat, organized, and clean. I'm very social I'll get to know peopl really fast. I never forget to do things.

Finding a well-crafted sentence like Goldstein's among the many papers rated *Unsatisfactory* or *Minimal* on the NAEP is less likely than spotting a polished diamond among chunks of anthracite hacked from an Appalachian coal mine. Viewing the link another way, any student who can devise and write such a sentence—who can sort through the information, pinpoint relationships, and express the ideas syntactically—has the thinking and writing skills needed to develop effective essays. One can hardly imagine a person writing such a sentence, yet being unable to write additional sentences to compose coherent paragraphs and papers. Such sentences are not bricks out of which buildings can be constructed but entire well-designed rooms reflecting mastery of materials and engineering which extends to broader applications as needed. This is confirmed by Mellon's finding that SC-test scores correlate highly with NAEP paper ratings.

One goal of SC exercises is to help students develop the reasoning and syntactical skills needed to write such sentences. SC aims to expand analytical ability from the level of simple-sentence thoughts to the capacity for comprehending, coordinating, and verbalizing relationships holding together many pieces of information.

Where SC has been properly used, it has proven beneficial. But because process-approach and WAC advocates have been so adamant and vocal in publicizing their procedures, many teachers are still relatively unacquainted with SC, and much work remains to be done developing good texts for all grade levels. This chapter extends Chapter 3 in discussing SC applications and issues.

Chapter 3 distinguished between cued and open SC. Cued exercises have built-in directions on how sentences should be combined— crossed out words should be deleted and capitalized words after sentences put in front, as in this example:

Officer Flubber collided with the tree out front. (AFTER . . .,)
Officer Flubber ran into the house. (HE . . .,)
Officer Flubber dived at the alleged thief. (. . .,)
Officer Flubber missed. (. . .,)
Officer Flubber sailed out the window. (AND)

After Officer Flubber collided with the tree out front, he ran into the house, dived at the alleged thief, missed, and sailed out the window.

By contrast, open exercises allow students options on combining, as in this exercise:

A writer with knowledge can find a job writing brochures.
The writer is skillful.
The knowledge is technical.
He or she can always find a job.
The job is high paying.
The brochures are commercial.
He or she may also write operating manuals.
This fact was reported in a newspaper article.

According to a newspaper article, a skillful writer with technical knowledge can always find a high-paying job writing commercial brochures and operating manuals.

While open exercises give students options on how they combine sentences, textbooks using them generally do not leave students without instructions and guidance. Patterns and examples for combining sentences are usually presented in the text before the exercises.

For example, in *Style and Readability in Technical Writing,* the first chapter is entitled "Combining with Addition/Deletion" and shows students examples of adding adjectives, adverbs, and prepositional phrases before asking them to combine sentences such as these:

The electrical arc produces light.
The arc is in a fluorescent tube.
The light is ultraviolet.
The ultraviolet light is invisible.

The electrical arc in a fluorescent tube produces invisible ultraviolet light.

The second chapter, entitled "Combining with the Wh-Connection," shows how information is added with *who, whose, which, whom,* and *that.* The third chapter shows how to handle appositives and, after several simpler exercises, lets students use everything learned so far to combine these sentences into one or two paragraphs.

The New Fuels

1. Most people have heard of gasohol.
   Gasohol is a blend.
   The blend is of gasoline.
   The blend is of alcohol.
2. You might even know that the alcohol comes from farm products.
   The alcohol is in this mixture.
3. But most people are not familiar with some other fuel mixes.
   The fuel mixes were recently created.
4. For example, how many of us know about petrocoal?
   Petrocoal is a combination.
   The combination is of gasoline with alcohol.
   The alcohol is made from coal.
   The alcohol is made from natural gas.
5. Or who could name the ingredients?
   The ingredients are in methacol.
   Methacol is a fuel.
   The fuel is recommended by the National Maritime Union.
   It is recommended for powering ships.
6. You might easily identify one ingredient by its name.
   The ingredient is methanol.

7. Yet, you would not likely guess the other ingredient.
    The ingredient is pulverized coal.
8. You would probably have the same trouble.
    The trouble is with Hydro Fuel.
    Hydro Fuel is a blend.
    The blend was created by United International Research, Inc.
9. You could predict that water is one element.
    The predicting would be from the name.
10. But the other two parts might elude you.
    One of the two parts is unleaded gasoline.
    One of the two parts is alcohol.
11. You would have an easier time, though.
    The easier time would be with Coco-Diesel.
    Coco-Diesel is coconut oil.
    Coco-Diesel is diesel fuel.
    Coco-Diesel is a mixture.
12. In this case, the name is a giveaway.
    It is a dead giveaway.
13. But only a short-order cook would have a chance with buckfry.
    buckfry is the last fuel on this list.
    Buckfry is a new fuel.
14. Who but a short-order cook would think of combining?
    The combining is of diesel fuel.
    The combining is with cooking oil.
    The cooking oil is recycled cooking oil.

Thus a student's ability to handle an increasing number of ideas and transformations is strengthened gradually.

Chapter 3 cites Argall's study in which students given intensive SC work showed significant decreases in garbled sentences, comma splices, sentence fragments, and other grammatical errors. Considering the nature of SC exercises, this is understandable. In SC students not only learn sentence patterns, but each time they write a combined sentence they are writing—from a model—correct spellings, subject-verb combinations, and other elements of usage.

Another attraction of SC is that it sidesteps the problem encountered in the process approach of students having nothing to write about, expressed in this excerpt from a student paper reprinted in the SC workbook *Writing Exercises: Building, Combining, and Revising:*

Sandy is sitting at her desk, nervously tugging at her frizzy hair and worrying about the essay she should have written for her English class. Three days ago she was given the assignment, and now the paper is due in just one hour. She uncaps her Bic, carefully prints her name at the top of the page, and then squeezes her eyes shut as she waits for inspiration.

Writing about summer vacations, embarrassing moments, and the adventures of a quarter has never been one of her favorite pastimes. She would rather be outside missing a bus (it would be less frustrating) or catching a cold (it would be more enjoyable).

. . .The blank sheet of paper stares at her, almost snickering it seems. She retaliates by defacing it with loops and squiggles and curlicues that puncture the paper. That accomplished, she glances at the clock; forty minutes to go.

The concern has been expressed that since SC exercises are directed at sentence-level manipulations, they might not improve the overall quality and organization of a student's papers. With open SC exercises that have students write complete paragraphs and papers, patterns of organization are modeled, models which students can use in their own writing. In fact, SC has an advantage over just having a student read model papers because it engages the student's attention actively, so that patterns and cohesion devices are seen more fully.

But even cued SC exercises, in spite of limiting the creative manipulation of sentences, seem to bring about improvements that reach beyond just the sentence level. O'Hare had an "experimental" group of students follow an intense cued-SC program with the following results:

> When eight experienced English teachers were asked to judge the overall writing quality of 30 pairs of experimental and control compositions, 60 compositions in all, that had been matched by sex and I.Q., they chose a significantly greater number of experimental compositions. Therefore, it was concluded that the experimental group wrote compositions that were significantly better in overall quality than the control group's compositions.

To be certain that students learn skills for writing complete papers, SC can be coupled with *inquiry* and *text reconstruction*. The TRC exercise entitled "The Company Needs A New Truck" in Chapter 5 shows students how to marshal support for an argument, while another exercise in the same chapter models the way details can be used to paint a verbal picture.

TRC also helps with elements of style. For example, Moffett worries that students may go sentence-combining crazy:

> [Students asked to subordinate one of the clauses in a dummy sentence, or to write a modifier-cluster sentence modeled on an example, often

get the idea that such constructions are *absolutely* good. At any rate, they will concoct them for no other motive than to comply with what seems to be the teacher's preference, just as they originally subordinated that clause to comply with the exercise directions, instead of doing so because their ideas demanded such a conjunction.

That SC can teach students the writing skill Moffett is concerned they may misuse shows it is certainly an improvement over much current writing instruction. Moreover, if Moffett's imagined misuse materializes, TRC can give students a perspective on balancing sentences for variety and pointed effect, as Kesey does here.

> Before the Reagan Administration cut off liberal money to the arts and humanities, I traveled around to a lot of posh little writing-teaching gigs. They'd fly you in, you'd get a pile of manuscripts to look over and a bunch of students. After some seminars and receptions, you'd take your check and fly home.
>
> The money was good, the hours short, the lime-light sweet. But when I look back and try to figure out, "What exactly did I *teach* those people?" the only thing that stands out occurred, I think, at a weekend fiction workshop somewhere in Texas. Thirty students had been picked by the regents—not on their ability, I gradually found out, but according to how much money their families had donated to the university.
>
> One of these chosen 30 was a nervous, blue-haired old lady; she had given a lot of money to the history wing of the library, one of the regents confided before he introduced her. She was known throughout the country as a philanthropist, activist and amateur anthropologist. But I discerned at once that what she wanted to be known as, above all, was a writer. You can't mistake those burning eyes. . . .

Kesey punctuated the last sentence as shown. It is not feasible through SC to teach all sentence patterns, punctuation possibilities, and other nuances of style. SC lays the foundation. TRC—a type of magical looking glass which lets you fully appreciate craftsmanship by seeing the writing styles of others as your own—opens imagination to the excitement of structuring language for creating sensual and emotional effects beyond literal meaning. Here is a set of Nordquist's sentences followed by an acceptable combination based on SC principles—and then Steinbeck's perfect beginning for "The Flood."

> The clouds marched in from the ocean.
> They were gray.
> They marched brokenly.
> They marched over the high coast mountains.
> They marched over the valleys.

> They came in puffs.
> They came in folds.
> They came in gray crags.
> They piled in together.
> They settled low over the west.

The gray clouds marched brokenly in from the ocean, over the high coast mountains, over the valleys—in puffs, folds, and gray crags—piling in together to settle low over the west.

The gray clouds marched brokenly in from the ocean and over the high coast mountains, and over the valleys, in puffs, in folds, in high crags, and they piled in together and they settled low over the west.

—John Steinbeck

If you try writing Steinbeck's version from memory, you may see in greater detail how an artist can combine words unconventionally to create the rhythm of cloud movement within a description of clouds piling up before a flood. And sometime later at an appropriate place in your own writing you may see a rhythm take form representing your subject, perhaps even causing you to recall your teacher and smile a thanks. SC builds craftsmanship. TRC gives a magnified picture of how craftsmanship is turned to artistry.

Finally, in writing both SC chapters, we benefited greatly from the comprehensive review Strong presents in *Creative Approaches to Sentence Combining.* However, because of misconceptions about stimulating creativity, Strong falters in recognizing the full power of SC for building workaday prose skills and stops short of recommending it as the major component for a composition course—even after quoting the positive results obtained in the SC-intensive studies by Daiker, et al. and O'Hare. Strong's position brings to mind Colby's observation that "Instructors who stress creativity over format and enthusiasm over mechanical accuracy are questioned by practitioners who point to the real-world need to communicate effectively in academic, employment, and life contexts". Strong's SC workbooks, along with several other workbooks in the field, suffer somewhat the same flaw. To save readers confusion, we are not recommending Strong's review, *Creative Approaches to Sentence Combining,* in this book. But we are indebted to his graceful, informative writings.

CHAPTER 11

A House Divided: Literature Versus Writing

The history of the teaching of writing and of literature in this country is reminiscent of both Lincoln's "House Divided" speech and Humpty-Dumpty's condition after his fall. Ironically, in spite of the fact that most English teachers teach both writing and literature, relations between the two areas have been strained for years.

For example, a headline in *Composition Chronicle* in September, 1989, states, "MLA's Commission on Writing and Literature ends work 'in a spirit of cautious optimism.' " The sub-headline continues "[The] Commission expresses hope for improved conditions for composition teaches, friendlier relations between composition and literature," and then asks, "but can the two fields really dance together?" Gere, in an October, 1989, article in *College English* uses stronger language, speaking of "gestures of rapprochement" between the two groups, "awkwardness," and the "chasm" that divides them. But Robertson used even more forceful language about the division between freshman composition instructors and literature professors, at the March, 1989 College Composition and Communication Conference:

> In higher education, if you're not in the catalogue, you're not a discipline or an art. We're not in the catalogue even though rhetoric has a rich intellectual history—a longer history than the other disciplines, and one that includes a substantive social purpose. . . .
>
> We are asking English departments to list in their section of the catalogue the courses we wish to offer as a curriculum in rhetoric. But the last

thing English departments would want to do now is to change our status as teachers-of-a-skill because for so long, the skills course called by the generic name Freshman English has been the goose that lays the Golden Eggs for English departments.

How did this situation come about? Assuming Robertson's assertions are true, how did literature get the upper hand over writing, or more broadly, rhetoric? A look at the history of the teaching of English, of both writing and literature, gives the answer.

It was not until 1876 that the first Professorship of English was created (by Harvard, for Child). Before that time professorships of rhetoric and oratory were the norm. Rhetoric deals with persuasion. In classical times it focused on the effective organization of content in orations. In medieval times and during the Middle Ages, rhetoric was one part of the academic trivium, the other two being grammar and logic. Now it is studied in both composition and speech (in the forms of debate and oration).

The current battle between literature and writing in this country can be traced from Colonial days. The emphasis on the teaching of literature, or more specifically, belles lettres (imaginative literature including fiction, criticism, drama, poetry, and essays) dates back to the influences of college on secondary schools. It all started when, in 1785 and 1788 respectively, Blair's *Lectures of Rhetoric and Belles Lettres* was adopted by Yale and Harvard as their standard rhetoric text. The measure of the importance of this book is that it was used by both colleges and secondary schools in America until the end of the 19th century. Its stress upon the morality exemplified by the belles lettres was particularly appealing to its users. Our struggling republic welcomed the combination of the morality taught in the belles lettres and the persuasion taught in rhetoric.

Harvard College became the rhetorical model for other colleges when in 1806 it established the Boylston Professorship of Rhetoric and Oratory, a lead it consolidated under the leadership of Channing, who occupied this chair from 1819–1851. In his 32-year tenure Channing set the pattern for the teaching of rhetoric nationally through:

1. a continuing emphasis on the belles lettres
2. a continuing emphasis on the psychological basis of persuasion
3. a shift from speaking practice to writing practice
4. more weight given to literary models
5. an insistence on correctness, based on grammar, style, and organization rules

6. increased use of rules for correct grammar, organization, and style, based on rules derived from literary models

In 1866 another important influence on the teaching of writing appeared, Bain's *English Composition and Rhetoric: A Manual*. This work introduced a rhetorical model widely used in teaching writing on both college and secondary levels, the four modes of discourse: description, narration, exposition, and argumentation. These four modes heavily influenced writing instruction until the mid-20th century and still appear in both college and secondary school composition textbooks. In fact, half of the 375 English departments surveyed in a Ford Foundation study reported their freshman composition courses are still organized around these modes, states Larson.

Not until the time of Child, Channing's successor in the Boylston Professorship, did the great schism between writing and literature develop on the college level, later to trickle down to secondary schools. When Child assumed the professorship, the main purpose of the English department, as it had been for years, was to teach writing. All college students were required to take three years of writing, during their sophomore, junior, and senior years. It was assumed that these elite students who were preparing for the professions of the church, law, and medicine needed such instruction. But, during the final quarter of the 19th century, social, political, cultural, and economic forces brought about a complete change in emphasis in teaching in college English departments from the teaching of writing to the teaching of literature.

Child, a German-university-trained philologist, accepted the Boylston Professorship with the idea of shifting the emphasis from writing to literature. Resentful of the time-consuming job of marking papers, he delegated it to lesser members of the department and expanded the university's literature courses. Johns Hopkins, the first American university to model itself after the German university organization, offered Child a position in 1876. To keep Child on the staff at Harvard, the administration established the first Professorship of English, appointed him to it, and set the stage for literature to replace writing as the main focus in English departments throughout the country. From 1876–1896, Child devoted his time to creating a new English literature program at Harvard while his successor as Boylston Professor, Hill, carried on the tradition of teaching composition through the application of rules. However, Child's Professorship of English was dominant with the Boylston Professorship a secondary appointment.

Child was able to put his plans into effect because of powerful forces in operation at that time. The focus of a university education had changed. No longer was such an education solely devoted to preparing members of three professions: clergymen, medical doctors, and lawyers. The expansion of America demanded training for other middle-class professionals who needed certification, those in fields from agriculture and engineering to education and social work. University doors opened wider, wide enough to admit students who met admission requirements, not just the elite.

English teachers, too, needed certification as a discipline. Philology and literary history provided the legitimate grounds for establishing literature as a scholarly discipline. Johns Hopkins led the way by offering graduate work in English literature and awarding its first literature doctorate in 1878. It, along with other institutions, was completing its move away from the classical curriculum. Four years earlier, in 1874, Harvard had taken a decisive step toward establishing the legitimacy of literature when prospective freshmen were required to take an essay test with the subject taken from works of English literature. This requirement not only helped establish literature as the subject matter of English but also forced the responsibility for teaching writing onto high schools, an effort that spared college professors from the drudgery of teaching composition while saving money for Harvard. Influenced by the prestige of Harvard, other institutions fell into step and did likewise. Literature, which had been used as exercise materials for teaching grammar and rhetoric in the 18th century, became firmly established as a subject of study in both high schools and colleges by the beginning of the 20th century.

Although these changes benefitted English departments and saved money as well, one small detail remained obvious. Entering college freshmen were not prepared to handle the demands of university writing. Something had to be done. And it was. First, the Harvard Board of Overseers, outraged by the poor writing revealed in the 1894 essay entrance examination, had the essays published, then denounced the high school English teachers responsible for turning out such inept student writers, a tradition of shifting blame that has continued down to the present.

Next, because college students needed to be taught to write and freshman composition was the bread-and-butter course of English departments, required freshman composition remained in the curriculum as a service course. Ironically, this lowly, despised course subsidizes prestigious departmental literature studies. Besides, it handily provides employment at bargain basement prices for faculty spouses, graduate students working on advanced degrees, and recent PhD graduates without much chance of finding tenured-track appointments.

What are the consequences of literature's dominating English departments? According to Bain, professor of English at the University of North Carolina at Chapel Hill, most university graduate programs of English are under the control "of the aristocrats whose ideas about literary study have always been more European than American and whose allegiances are to those nineteenth-century European models upon which most English graduate schools are based." And, since those aristocrats are more interested in literary research, writing articles and books, and graduate studies programs than in preparing community college, secondary school, and elementary school English teachers, the teaching of writing has suffered in many ways:

1. Bachelor's and master's degree holders have gone into school and community college classrooms untrained to teach basic writing to students.
2. Self-taught master secondary school writing teachers moved up to community college teaching, depriving beginning, younger teachers of curriculum aid and role models.
3. English graduate schools more or less abandoned working with secondary schools.
4. English and education departments severed ties and relinquished responsibility for training classroom teachers.
5. English departments and their institutions respond more and more to fashionable crises in their field in efforts to appear accountable and to secure funding, including areas such as Writing across the Curriculum, cultural literacy, neglecting various priorities such as aiding minorities and preparing vocational/technical students for gainful employment.

McCleary, founder and editor of *Composition Chronicle,* provides a personal perspective on the situation in recalling his experiences in 1974 at the University of Texas, Austin. He and his wife wanted to do their doctoral studies under Kinneavy, distinguished rhetorician and composition expert:

At the time he [Kinneavy] held a joint appointment in English and in English Education; we enrolled in English Education because the English Department was not hospitable to the study of composition/rhetoric. (It still isn't, despite now having its own doctoral program in rhetoric and employing some very fine rhetoricians including Maxine Hairston, Lester Faigley, and John Ruszkiewicz. The story of Kinneavy's travails with that department could occupy a whole issue of *Composition Chronicle.*)

To show just how poorly prepared undergraduate English majors are for teaching, consider the results of a 1987 survey done by Stewart, Kansas State University Professor of English, former head of the Conference on College Composition and Communication, prolific author, and eminent leader in rhetoric and composition. Stewart's study covers "the undergraduate English major programs of 194 American colleges and universities . . . located in all 50 states and the District of Columbia . . . public and private universities, land grant institutions, former teachers' colleges, and private liberal arts colleges," representative of all types of institutions that offer undergraduate majors in English.

His three-part, 18-month study includes school catalogues, course syllabi, and enrollment figures in various types of programs. He classified the programs offered English majors into three major categories:

1. "Straight literature programs or those so predominantly literature that modifications in them are insignificant." (11 of 194 programs)
2. Emphasis upon literary studies offering "majors courses in creative writing, linguistics, and, occasionally, composition and rhetoric." (107 of 194 programs)
3. Programs offering "an option in creative writing or rhetoric and composition . . . a block of courses which students take, in lieu of a certain number of literature courses."

Stewart also reports the following enrollment figures in various English department categories in the 108 schools who replied to his requests for such statistics:

Literature—21,622
Teacher certification—3,653
Composition and Rhetoric—1,647
Creative Writing—1,094
Linguistics—insignificant

He concludes from these results that:

. . . most students perceive the majors to be a program of study concentrating on the analysis of literature. . . . Canon reform is becoming a significant question in a number of programs, but no matter how it is resolved, the focus of the program is still on the study of literature. . . . and, unfortunately . . ., in the total number of English majors for which

I have reports, the disparity between the number in the literature concentration and the others is striking.

Not surprisingly, he calls for a reform of the literature major, with a total of 39 semester hours, "13 three-hour courses; eight in literature, two in language and linguistics, one in creative writing, and two in composition and rhetoric," stating that students need composition history and theory courses just as much as they need similar literature courses. Second, other than these required courses, he suggests adding options in creative writing, language and linguistics, and composition and rhetoric, thereby adding more hours to the major for students electing these options. He concludes by quoting Fred Scott's 1900 "Report on College Entrance Requirements in English":

> Are our methods of instruction in English in harmony with the social demands of our great industrial community? I suspect that they are not. More than that I suspect that the hard knot of the English question lies right here—that our present ideals and methods of instruction are in large part remnants of an adaptation to a state of things which long since passed away.

Stewart's findings and recommendations are reflected in a May 1989 of *Composition Chronicle,* which calls "the status of composition . . . a puzzlement at all levels" and declares that "until it is straightened out at the higher levels of education, where teachers of all the other levels are trained, we will continue to have a curious situation throughout the land." Doubtless, proficiency in writing is valued, as evidenced by state and local policies of widespread testing of skills in writing, required remedial writing courses, and required composition courses at the post-secondary level. However, training for writing teachers at all levels, elementary through university, is top-heavy in literature with non-existent or little preparation for the teaching of writing. English teachers at all levels are prepared by departments that lack tenured writing specialists. Undergraduates are taught by "the underprepared and/or those without regular professional status," according to an article, "The Push to Upgrade Composition. . . ."

How did the "democrats," according to Bain—who "see the mission of the English department as teaching young men and women how to read and to write critically and effectively" and also "believe their departments have some obligations to (prepare) teachers of reading and writing"—permit the "aristocrats" to gain the upper hand?

In a sense the democrats were caught in a culture lag. They had no discipline to ally themselves with because their former allegiance to classical studies and rhetoric was rendered obsolete by the shift to English language and literature. Like their modern composition-teacher counterparts, they lacked power because they were committed to undergraduate teaching, and, worse yet, to an undergraduate skills course. In short, rhetoric as a subject for graduate study was inconceivable. Overworked and underpaid, they were no match for the juggernaut of literary scholars buttressed by the power of their newly established discipline with its authoritative base in German-university-type graduate schools of English. Moreover, once entrenched and in control of the training of English teachers, the aristocrats expanded their domain into secondary schools by requiring college entrance essay examinations based on lists of works by English literature, thereby mandating the secondary school English curriculum.

In spite of the seeming invincible position of the aristocrats, the democrats fought back. More and more of them, both at the college and secondary levels, rebelled against the power of the Harvard-type required reading lists. By 1911 there were enough democrats to form the National Council of Teachers of English (NCTE) and to begin publishing in 1912 the *English Journal*. These were part of their answer to the aristocrats of the Modern Language Association who considered the only worthwhile scholarship to be literary studies. The first president of the NCTE and former president of the MLA, Fred Scott of the University of Michigan, a literary scholar himself, joined the democrats in supporting the teaching of writing. In 1914 college speech teachers, who had continued to teach the history of rhetoric, left the NCTE and started the National Association for Academic Teachers of Public Speaking which later became the Speech Communication Association.

The progressive education movement also opposed the aristocrats. Rejecting the elitism inherent in required reading lists, the progressives stressed social aspects of education, preparing students to be worthwhile citizens, and attempting to meet individual student needs. Progressives strived to cut the tie between the standard canon of literature and writing and substitute meaningful assignments, but their efforts were in vain, at least at the college level, where freshman composition continued to be an introduction to literature and the writing of literary essays. The few actual writing courses in existence followed the four forms of discourse presented in Bain's 1866 textbook.

Although in the 1930s, the New Criticism marked a movement away from a literary history approach to scholarship, substituting close textual analysis of works, the teaching of writing remained pretty much unchanged until the 1950s. However, in the early 1940s the

New Criticism appeared to offer a way of uniting the divided house of English by basing writing courses on the subject that English teachers know best, literature. Further, the teachers wouldn't become burned-out "composition slaves" since they would be stimulated intellectually by constant work with great literature. Moreover, it offered bonuses for students as well because it automatically gave them subjects to write about while exposing them to the liberating effects of classic ideas and self-expressive works of the literary canon. Finally, at the time of the Cold War, literary-based composition provided a noncontroversial refuge, especially if the teaching of literature could be shown to enhance the democratic way of life.

But an overview of what happened to the relationship between literature and writing cannot be divided into neat compartments, each following the other in impeccable time order; for at the same time the New Criticism was influencing the teaching of writing, other forces were in operation. General education, core courses, and communications all influenced the teaching of writing during the period from approximately the early 1940s on into the 1960s. Core courses cut across department lines with the composition core serving as the tool for knowledge acquisition in other core areas of general education— biological, physical, and social sciences, and the humanities. A variation of this core approach, the cooperative approach, has team teaching with, for example, an English teacher working with a teacher from another discipline, both responsible for the same group of students. The theory was admirable but, according to Russell, in practice "few [programs] incorporated writing instruction in any systematic way, focusing instead on the reading of literature."

Communications courses were developed during World War II when officer candidates needed a speeded-up education. Therefore, speaking and writing were not taught as separate classes but combined with other courses. By 1947 the communications movement was important enough to warrant a conference organized jointly by the NCTE and the Speech Association of America. The next year the Conference on College Composition and Communication was organized, and in 1950 its journal, *College Composition and Communication,* was founded. But by the 1960s, except for a few isolated programs such as that at the State University of Iowa, as Russell points out, the movement had lost its impetus: "the communications caboose of the CCCC became unhitched, and the organization chugged on toward rhetoric and other more glamorous destinations." The House Divided remained filled with its squabbling children, and literature remained dominant in writing courses.

One area remains to be examined. What does research through the years tell us about the efficacy of using literature to teach writing? Considering how widely literature is taught, one might expect to find volumes of studies on different aspects of using literature to improve writing skills. Instead, there are virtually no studies.

For example, in *Research in Written Composition*, the major review of writing research published by the National Council of Teaching of English, the index lists twenty-four references on the effects of teaching grammar on writing. In contrast, under the heading *literature,* not one reference is found. Under *literary devices, use of,* one page is cited. On that page two studies are reported about the use of "alliteration, hyperbole, metaphor, simile, and personification in young children's writing." A check of the heading *Models, of writing* yields six references, but only two studies dealing with literature are discussed. Both deal with grade school children who either read children's literature themselves or had it read to them by teachers, in contrast to control groups with "no planned literary program"; the results on their writing were "so mixed to the extent that they are difficult to interpret." Not much help there.

Another likely source of relevant evidence is the literature article in the latest edition of the *Encyclopedia of Educational Research.* Here research surprises continue. No direct studies of the effect of literature instruction on writing skills are reported. The literary studies reported are in these areas: status surveys, reading interests, responses to literature, and instructional techniques. The best overall picture that we have of the effect of teaching literature on writing skills is a summary statement in the previously cited NCTE research survey:

> What I have referred to as teaching from models undoubtedly has a place in the English program. This research indicates that emphasis on the presentation of good pieces of writing as models is significantly more useful than the study of grammar. At the same time, treatments which use the study of models almost exclusively are less effective than other available techniques.)

CHAPTER 12

Un-Shotgunning
and De-Pack Ratting

Physical fitness experts recommend that, for cardiovascular health, a person should build up to a program of twenty-five minutes of vigorous exercise four times a week. Unfortunately for busy people, however, absolutely no physical benefits are gained from performing twenty-five minutes of vigorous exercise just once a week. In fact, vigorous exercise performed just once a week can precipitate a heart attack. A little bit of a useful activity is not necessarily a little useful.

Burying a few useful writing exercises among piles of useless ones, as is done in numerous English textbooks, is not an effective pedagogy for building writing skills. Many English texts use the shotgun approach to program design. Publishers make sure to include a few exercises of virtually every type found in all other textbooks and programs so that whatever approach a teacher favors, their textbook salesman can show where that approach is "covered" in their text.

The shotgun method promises to be of at least some benefit by blasting a student with everything that could possibly hit the mark of improving skills. However, the charging bull elephant of illiteracy requires more than a shotgun. Students need many hours of "time on task" with powerful illiteracy fighters such as sentence combining.

We recently reviewed a newly published edition of a popular high school English text to see how much SC it includes. SC is squeezed into the grammar section of the text, which spans pages 282–405. Among these 123 pages, 6 pages are on SC, 23 on diagraming sentences, and the rest are on grammatical terminology with accompanying exercises. A teacher using such a text might feel he or she is giving his or her students SC training. But there is not enough of it. A truck runs no better with one wheel than with no wheels—it needs all four. Textbooks which have one wheel of SC and the other three wheels of grammar, process instruction, and literature surveys—with a spare tire of WAC—will not carry students through the toll gates of writing examinations and on to their destinations of careers in a technological world requiring full-powered communication skills.

Pack ratting is a related flaw of many textbooks to be avoided. The pack-rat syndrome is the compulsion to keep at least a small sample of old things even after new ones have been developed to replace them—a commendable attitude for historical societies but not textbook authors. Leafing through many English textbooks is, in effect, taking a historical tour of teaching materials for a century or more. Mid-19th century modes of discourse are jostled by 1970s freewriting, expressive writing, and journals. Diagramming and the parts of speech are time-warped around SC. Communication chapters involving speaking and listening skills coexist with business writing and college application forms. Traditional research papers inhabit a chapter or more while students are also exposed briefly to techniques for writing ancient Japanese poetry, short stories, one-act plays, TV scripts, and modern commercials.

Giving students a broad exposure to various forms of writing is a praiseworthy educational goal, but the road to poor writing skills is papered with programs having impeccable intentions. The road also has been decorated with billboards like *the writing process, cultural literacy, writing-across-the-curriculum,* and *thinking skills.* Publishers print these boldly on their advertising brochures and textbook covers, then between the covers give just little dabs of each, implying that, like Brylcreme, "a little dab'll do ya." But teaching writing is a hairier problem than calming a cowlick and requires more than just dabs of this and that.

SC, inquiry training, and text reconstruction—while seen by some as too "mechanistic" and not "natural" or "humanistic"—have proven to be effective skill builders. Textbooks focusing on such methods without other distractions may not appear to be as much fun as the sampler packages. But because they work, they tend to be more rewarding for both teachers and students.

Bibliography

Chapter 1

Applebee, A. N., Langer, J. A., & Mullis, I. V. S. *The Writing Report Card: Writing Achievement in American Schools* (Report No. 15-W-02). Princeton, NJ: Educational Testing Service, 1986.

Businesses Teaching Workers 3 R's. *The New York Times,* 1 May 1988: 1, 15.

Cohen, M. The New Illiteracy: It's America's Dirty Little Secret. *The Boston Globe,* 24 May 1987: 1A.

Franklin, B. *Poor Richard's Almanac.* Philadelphia: 1732–1757.

Perot, H. R. Education for the Year 2000. *The Seattle Times,* 4 Dec. 1988: 20A. (Reprinted from *The Washington Post*)

William T. Grant Foundation Commission on Work, Family, and Citizenship. The forgotten half: Non-college-bound youth in America. *Phi Delta Kappan,* Feb., 1988: 409–414.

Chapter 2

Braddock, R., R. Lloyd-Jones, & L. Schoer. *Research in Written Composition.* Urbana, IL: National Council of Teachers of English, 1963.

From Book 7. "Silver Burdett English K-8: Setting the New Standard." Brochure. Lexington, Mass.: Silver Burdett & Ginn, 1989.

Harris, R. J. "An Experimental Inquiry into the Functions and Value of Formal Grammar in the Teaching of English, with Special Reference to the Teaching of Correct Written English to Children, Aged Twelve to Fourteen." Diss., University of London, 1962.

Hillocks, George, Jr. *Research in Written Composition.* Urbana, IL: ERIC Clearinghouse on Reading and Communications Skills/National Conference on Research in English, 1986.

Petrosky, Anthony R. "Grammar Instruction: What We Know," *English Journal* December 1977:

Chapter 3

Argall, Rebecca S. "Sentence Combining: An Incisive Tool for Proofreading." Paper Presented at the Annual Meeting of the Conference on College Composition and Communication. San Francisco, Calif. 18–20 Mar. 1982.

Cooper, Charles R. "An Outline for Writing Sentence-Combining Problems," *English Journal* 62 (Jan 1973): 96–102, 108.

Cooper, Thomas C., Genelle Morain, and Theodore Kalivorda. *Sentence Combining in Second Language Instruction.* Language in Education: Theory and Practice, No. 31. Washington, D.C.: Center for Applied Linguistics, 1980.

Daiker, Donald A., Andrew Kerek, and Max Morenberg. *The Writer's Options: College Sentence Combining.* New York: Harper & Row, 1979.

Elbow, Peter. "The Challenge for Sentence Combining." *Sentence Combining: A Rhetorical Perspective.* Eds. Donald A. Daiker, Andrew Kerek, and Max Morenberg. Carbondale, Ill.: Southern Illinois University Press, 1985.

Emig, Janet. *The Composing Processes of Twelfth Graders.* National Council of Teachers of English, Report No. 13. Urbana, Ill.: National Council of Teachers of English, 1971.

Gebhardt, Richard. Sentence Combining in the Teaching of the Writing Process. In *Sentence Combining: A Rhetorical Perspective,* ed. by Donald A. Daiker, Andrew Kerek, and Max Morenberg. Carbondale, IL: Southern Illinois University Press, 1985.

Hillocks, George, Jr. *Research in Written Composition.* Urbana, IL: ERIC Clearinghouse on Reading and Communications Skills/National Conference on Research in English, 1986.

Jones, Mary Ann C. "An Investigation to Determine the Syntactic Growth as a Result of Sentence-Combining Practice in Freshman English." Diss. Auburn University, 1980.

Kerek, Andrew, Donald A. Daiker, and Max Morenberg. "Sentence Combining and College Composition." *Perceptual and Motor Skills* 51 (1980): 1059–1157.

McAfee, Deurelle C. "Effect of Sentence-Combining Instruction on the Reading and Writing Achievement of Fifth-Grade Children in a Suburban School District." Diss. Texas Woman's University, 1980.

Mellon, John C. "Issues in the Theory and Practice of Sentence Combining: A Twenty Year Perspective." *Sentence Combining and the Teaching of Writing: Selected Papers from the Miami University Conference.* Eds. Donald A. Daiker, Andrew Kerek, and Max Morenberg. Conway, Ark.: L & S Books, 1979.

Ney, J. W. "The Hazards of the Course: Sentence-Combining in Freshman English." *The English Record* Summer-Autumn 1976a: 70–77.

O'Hare, Frank. *Sentence Combining: Improving Student Writing Without Formal Grammar Instruction.* Urbana, Ill.: National Council of Teachers of English, 1973.

Stoddard, Elizabeth P. "The Combined Effect of Creative Thinking and Sentence-Combining Activities on the Writing Ability of Above Average Fifth and Sixth Grade Students." Diss. University of Connecticut, 1982.

Whimbey, Arthur. *Analytical Reading & Reasoning.* 2nd ed. Stamford, Conn.: Innovative Sciences, 1990.

Whimbey, Arthur, and Elizabeth Lynn Jenkins. *Analyze, Organize, Write.* Rev. ed. Hillsdale, N.J.: Lawrence Erlbaum Associates, 1987.

Whimbey, Arthur, and Jack Lochhead. *Problem Solving and Comprehension.* 4th ed. Hillsdale, N.J.: Lawrence Erlbaum Associates, 1988.

Chapter 4

Anderson, Joann Romeo, et al. *Integrated Skills Reinforcement: Reading, Writing, Speaking, and Listening Across the Curriculum.* Longman Series in College Composition and Communications. New York: Longman, 1983.

Applebee, Arthur N., Janet A. Langer, and Ina V. S. Mullis. *The Writing Report Card: Writing Achievement in American Schools,* Report No. 15-W-02. Princeton, N. J.: Educational Testing Service, 1986.

Bendixen, Alfred. "There Goes the Cave." Rev. of *Caverns,* by Robert Blucher, et al. *New York Times Book Review* 21 Jan. 1990: 28–29.

Emig, Janet. *The Composing Processes of Twelfth Graders.* National Council of Teachers of English, Report No. 13. Urbana, Ill.: National Council of Teachers of English, 1971.

Graves, Richard L. "The Sentence: A Reluctant Medium." *Rhetoric and Composition: A Sourcebook for Teachers and Writers.* New ed. Upper Montclair, N.J.: Boynton/Cook, 1984. 93–94.

Hillocks, George, Jr. *Research in Written Composition.* Urbana, Ill.: ERIC Clearinghouse on Reading and Communications Skills/National Conference on Research in English, 1986.

Hoffer, Eric. "May 11." *Working and Thinking on the Waterfront.* New York: Harper & Row, 1969.

Kelly, Lou. "Toward Competence and Creativity in an Open Class." *College English* 34 (1973): 644–660.

Murray, Donald M. "Teach Writing as a Process not Product." *The Leaflet* Nov. 1972: 11–14. Rpt. in *Rhetoric and Composition: A Sourcebook for Teachers and Writers.* New ed. Ed. Richard L. Graves. Upper Montclair, N.J.: Boynton/Cook, 1984. 89–94.

Shaw, Harry Edmund. "Responding to Student Essays." *Teaching Prose: A Guide for Writing Instructors.* Eds. Fredric V. Bogel and Katherine K. Gottschalk. New York: W. W. Norton, 1984.

Trimmer, Joseph F., and James M. McCrimmon. *Writing with a Purpose.* Short 9th ed. Boston: Houghton Mifflin, 1988.

Chapter 5

Applebee, Arthur N., Langer Judith A., and Ina V. S. Mullis. *The Writing Report Card: Writing Achievement in American Schools,* Report No. 15-W-02. Princeton, N.J.: Educational Testing Service, 1986.

Baldwin, Thomas W. *William Shakespere's Small Latin & Less Greek.* 2 vols. Urbana, Ill.: University of Illinois, 1944.

Doctorow, E. L. "The Great Oakland Earthquake." Rev. of *Letters of Jack London*. Eds. Earle Labor, Robert C. Leitz, 3rd, and I. Milo Shepard, and *American Dreamers: Carmian and Jack London* by Clarice Stasz. *New York Times Book Review* 11 Dec. 1988: 1, 39, 41–42.

Franklin, Benjamin. *Autobiography of Benjamin Franklin*. Harvard Classics I. Ed. Charles Eliot. New York: P. F. Collier & Son, 1909.

Friedmann, T. and J. MacKillop. *Copy Book: Mastering Basic Grammar and Style*. New York: Holt, Rinehart, and Winston, 1980.

Gorrell, D. "Controlled Composition for Basic Writers." *College Composition and Communication* 32 (1981): 308–16.

Jones, James. *To Reach Eternity: The Letters of James Jones*. Ed. George Hendrick. New York: Random House, 1989.

Langan, John. *English Skills*, 3rd ed. New York: McGraw-Hill, 1985.

Levy, Wilbert J. *Paragraph Play*. New York: Amsco, 1985.

Linden, Myra J., and Arthur Whimbey. *Analytical Writing and Thinking: Facing the Tests*. Hillsdale, N.J.: Lawrence Erlbaum Associates, 1990.

Lundquizt, James. *Jack London: Adventures, Ideas, and Fiction*. New York: Ungar, 1987.

MacShane, F. *Into Eternity: The Life of James Jones: American Writer*. Boston: Houghton Mifflin, 1985.

Malcolm X. *Autobiography of Malcolm X*. New York: Ballantine, 1977.

Maugham, W. Somerset. *The Summing Up*. New York: Penguin, 1978.

Morton, Elaine. "Integrating Cognitive Skills into a Developmental Reading Course." *Issues in College Learning Centers: Abstracts of Papers at the Eighth National Conference on College Learning Centers*. Long Island University, May 1986.

Roen, Duan R. "Coherence in Writing." *English Journal* Aug. 1984: 36.

Whimbey, Arthur, and Elizabeth Lynn Jenkins. *Analyze, Organize, Write*. Rev. ed. Hillsdale, N.J.: Lawrence Erlbaum Associates, 1987.

Chapter 6

Anderson, Joann Romeo, et al. *Integrated Skills Reinforcement: Reading, Writing, Speaking, and Listening Across the Curriculum*. Longman Series in College Composition and Communications. New York: Longman, 1983.

Blanc, Robert. School of Medicine, University of Missouri, Kansas City, Missouri. 64110-2499.

Bloom, Benjamin, S., and Lois J. Broder. *Problem-Solving Processes of College Students*. Chicago: University of Chicago Press, 1950.

Brown, Karen. Fort Meade Senior High School, Fort Meade, Florida.

Couch, Ruth. "Dealing with Objections to Writing Across the Curriculum." *Teaching English in the Two-Year College* 16 (1989): 193–96.

Fulwiler, Toby E. "Journal Writing Across the Curriculum." *How to Handle the Paper Load*. Urbana, Ill.: National Council of Teachers of English, 1979–80.

Glassman, Steve. "The Light Touch: Minimal Applications of the Partner Approach to Writing Across the Curriculum." *Florida English Journal* Spring 1989: 22–26.

Heiman, Marsha, and Slomianko, Joshua. *Critical Thinking Skills.* Washington, D.C.: National Education Association, 1985.

Heiman, Marsha, and Slomianko, Joshua. *Methods of Inquiry.* Cambridge, Mass.: Learning to Learn, 1987.

Jordan, Diane Martin, and Michael Moorhead. "Writing Across the Curriculum: The Mentor Project." *Teaching English in the Two-Year College* 16 (1989): 99–103.

Langer, Judith A., and Arthur N. Applebee. *How Writing Shapes Thinking: A Study of Teaching and Learning.* National Council of Teachers of English, Research Report No. 22. Urbana, Ill.: National Council of Teachers of English, 1987.

Lochhead, Jack. Cognitive Process Research Group, University of Massachusetts, Amherst, Massachusetts 01003.

Luria, Alexander R. The Development of Writing in the Child. *Soviety Psychology* 16: 65–114.

Moss, Andrew, and Carol Holder. *Improving Student Writing: A Guidebook for Faculty in All Disciplines.* Pomona, Ca.: California State Polytechnic University, 1988. Distributed by Kendall/Hunt Publishers.

Soven, Margot. "Critical Thinking: The Role of Writing Across the Curriculum Project Administrator." *Composition Chronicle* Oct. 1989: 8–9.

Spear, Karen. *Sharing Writing: Peer Response Groups in English Classes.* Portsmouth, N.H.: Boynton/Cook, 1988.

Stotsky, Sandra. "Research on Reading/Writing Relationships: A Synthesis and Suggested Directions." *Language Arts* 60 (1983): 627–642.

Thurber, James. Interview. George Plimpton and Max Steele. *Writers at Work: The Paris Review Interviews.* 1st Series. Ed. Malcolm Cowley. New York: Paris Review, 1957.

Toth, Marian Davies. "Definition of Writing to Learn." Association for Supervision and Curriculum Development National Curriculum Study Institutes. San Francisco, Calif. 26–28 July 1989.

Tuschudi, Stephen. "Writing and Learning—'Workaday' Writing." *Forms and Structures for Writing to Learn.* Handout of Marian Davies Toth. Association for Supervision and Curriculum Development National Curriculum Study Institutes, San Francisco, Calif. 26–28 July 1989.

Watson, James D. *The Double Helix.* New York: W. W. Norton, 1980.

Woods, Don. Department of Chemical Engineering, McMaster University, Hamilton, Ontario, Canada, L8S 417.

Chapter 8

Hillocks, George, Jr. "Inquiry." *Research in Written Composition.* Urbana, Ill.: ERIC Clearinghouse on Reading and Communication Skills/National Conference on Research in English, 1986. 180–86.

Linden, Myra J., and Arthur Whimbey. *Analytical Writing and Thinking: Facing the Tests.* Hillsdale, N.J.: Lawrence Erlbaum Associates, 1990.

Chapter 9

Colby, Anita Y., "Writing Instruction in the Two-Year College." *ERIC Digest.* Aug. 1986: 1–4.

Cooper, Charles R. "An Outline for Writing Sentence-Combining Problems." *English Journal* 62 (Jan. 1973): 96–102.

Linden, Myra J., and Arthur Whimbey. *Analytical Writing and Thinking: Facing the Tests.* Hillsdale, N.J.: Lawrence Erlbaum Associates, 1990.

Whimbey, Arthur, and Elizabeth Lynn Jenkins. *Analyze, Organize, Write.* Rev. ed. Hillsdale, N.J.: Lawrence Erlbaum Associates, 1987.

Chapter 10

Applebee, Arthur N., Langer, Judith A., and Ina V. S. Mullis. *The Writing Report Card: Writing Achievement in American Schools,* Report No. 15-W-02. Princeton, N.J.: Educational Testing Service, 1986.

Colby, Anita Y. "Writing Instruction in the Two-Year College," *ERIC Digest.* Aug. 1986: 1–4.

DeGeorge, James, Gary A. Olson, and Richard Ray. *Style and Readability in Technical Writing. A Sentence-Combining Approach.* New York: Random House, 1984.

Kesey, Ken. "Remember This: Write What You Don't Know." *New York Times Book Review* 31 Dec. 1989: 1, 21–22.

Moffett, James. *Teaching the Universe of Discourse.* Boston: Houghton Mifflin, 1968. 170–71.

Nordquist, Richard F. *Writing Exercises: Building, Combining and Revising.* New York: Macmillan, 1985.

O'Hare, Frank. *Sentence Combining: Improving Student Writing Without Formal Grammar Instruction.* NCTE Committee on Research, Report Series No. 15. Urbana, Ill.: National Council of Teachers of English, 1973.

Strong, William. *Creative Approaches to Sentence Combining.* Urbana, Ill.: ERIC Clearinghouse on Reading and Communication Skills and the National Council of Teachers of English, 1986.

Whimbey, Arthur, and Elizabeth Lynn Jenkins. *Analyze, Organize, Write.* Rev. ed. Hillsdale, N.J.: Lawrence Erlbaum Associates, 1987.

Chapter 11

Applebee, Arthur N. "Literature." *Encyclopedia of Educational Research.* 1982 ed.

Bain, Bob. "Attacking Ignorance and Apathy in High Places." *Teaching English in the Two-Year College* 15 (1988): 202–209.

Berlin, James A. *Rhetoric and Reality: Writing Instruction in American Colleges, 1900–1985.* Carbondale, Ill.: Southern Illinois University Press, 1987.

Gere, Anne Ruggles. "Review: Composition and Literature: The Continuing Conversation." *College English* 51 (1989): 617–22.

Gorrell, Robert M., Patricia Bizzell, and Bruce Herzberg. *The Bedford Bibliogra-*

phy for Teachers of Writing. New York: Bedford Books of St. Martin's Press, 1987.

Hillocks, George, Jr. *Research on Written Composition*. Urbana, Ill.: National Council of Teachers of English, 1986.

McCleary, Bill. "Influence of James L. Kinneavy and *A Theory of Discourse* continues to grow." *Composition Chronicle* April 1989: 1–2.

"MLA's Commission on Writing and Literature ends work 'in a spirit of cautious optimism.' " *Composition Chronicle* Sept. 1989: 1–2.

"The push to upgrade composition: An effort in which we *all* have a stake." *Composition Chronicle* May 1989: 6.

Larson, Richard C. In Robertson, Linda R. "Alliances Between Rhetoric and English: The Politics." *Composition Chronicle* May 1989: 5–7.

Robertson, Linda R. "Alliances Between Rhetoric and English: The Politics." *Composition Chronicle* May 1989: 5–7.

Russell, David R. "Writing Across the Curriculum in Historical Perspective: Toward a Social Interpretation." *College English* 52 (1990): 52–73.

Stewart, Donald C. "What Is an English Major, and What Should It Be?" *College Composition and Communication* 40 (1989): 188–202.

Index

Other books of related interest...